Tony

With Respect

AUTHORITY IN THE CATHOLIC CHURCH

the columba press

First published in 2008 by
the columba press
55A Spruce Avenue, Stillorgan Industrial Park,
Blackrock, Co Dublin

Cover by Bill Bolger
Origination by The Columba Press
Printed by Athenaeum Press Ltd, Gateshead

ISBN 978-1-85607-609-8

Table of Contents

To Jacinta
lover of truth and wisdom

Introduction

The title of this book *With Respect* was suggested to me by my good friend, Ned Prendergast. Over the years of our friendship Ned noticed that I had the habit of prefacing some of my most aggressive remarks with the words,'with respect'. The use of the phrase was an early warning indicator to him that a passionate onslaught of some kind was about to be launched and invariably it would include a severe critique of an issue or position that had been raised. In retrospect, I can chuckle and even chide myself about how easily I could reveal my convictions. Today I am much more alert about the use of the term and I am aware of the territory I enter when I choose to use it.

The same friend reminded me that authority is closely linked to respect which has its origins in the Latin *respicere* which means to see again or to see with new eyes. As I begin this examination of this subject, I have no doubt that my passionate convictions about some of the defects in authoritative structures within the Catholic Church will be evident. There is much that needs to be addressed. However, with equal conviction, I want to proclaim with deep gratitude the splendour of an informed and spiritual *magisterium*. The Holy Spirit has given me the grace to see with new eyes and to treasure the gift of authority which is one of God's perennial graces to his church.

This is a book about authority, especially authority as exercised in the Roman Catholic Church. I write as a practising Catholic who loves my church and feels called to serve in that church as fully as I can with whatever gifts that God has given to me. I write as someone privileged to have had access to academic training and ongoing formation throughout my life. I hold degrees in education and theology and have managed to acquire a wide and enriching portfolio of ministry, ranging from teacher in Africa, to school chaplain, from community founder to teacher of theology, from father of four wonderful young women to counsellor of many broken spirits, from husband with a devoted wife to writer on religious issues.

I write today because I struggle with authority as I believe many fellow church members, both cleric and lay, do. I have become mature enough to recognise that this is part of my own human weakness, the persistent need to soothe and mollify my own ego, not to bow the knee to another. Humility does not come easily to this particular soul! What I have learned from my own life experience is that authority comes not from titles or books or positions but from the quality of relationship. One may acquire titles and positions, they may have status in the local or global context but these are empty if the pursuant relationships with the subjects of that authority are not rich and respectful.

Authority spawns a number of associated terms or ideas and they are all part of the cultural mix which impacts on the discussions within this book. Some words that might spring readily to mind would be obedience, hierarchy, leadership, governance, dissent and conscience. Others that might not be so explicit could include words such as subsidiarity, charism, local and universal. In the course of this book, these are terms that I will seek to explicate because they all have a bearing on the outworkings of this term authority.

I see the church today, with all its difficulties, still throbbing with life. She is alive because God's Spirit continues to breathe life into her. Jesus promised the gift of the Spirit who would not leave us orphaned and the life force that beats gently or pulsates widely in so many facets of this wonderful mystery proclaims this vibrant presence.

The book is offered to all men and women who exercise, endure, rail against, submit to or grapple with authority. It is offered humbly and with respect.

CHAPTER 1

A Personal Shaping

Authority is a term I have been pondering for some time. For me it is a difficult word because I know instinctively my own hackles are aroused. I sense in it not something benign or helpful or pastoral but something of the tyrant, of the boss, of the *know your place* kind of put down. I know intellectually that there is another reality where authority is life-enhancing and freeing and this core dimension will be given due attention as this book unfolds. However, I must acknowledge from the outset a certain prickly irritation that surfaces in my gut as I begin this work.

Perhaps that unease has something to do with my Catholic upbringing in Northern Ireland where evidence of bigotry and sectarianism was a constant backdrop. My childhood was experienced and lived in a society where civic and political authority was seen as abusive and persistent. I had a nagging sense throughout those years that I didn't really belong within this part of the 'United Kingdom', that I was tolerated but not fully welcomed, that I lived here under suffrance, that the authority which watched over me and, more accurately, watched me, did not really trust me. I had the gnawing sense that I was under suspicion, that I was somehow beyond the pale, outside the inner circle, always on the edge, not really belonging. I sought another kind of authority, freer and more benign, idealistically conferred to the land across the border known as the 'Free State'.

Later, the formative years of my adolesence in the late 1960s were shaped in the context of a civil rights movement that was railing against injustice, gerrymandering and the abuse of authority by those who clung to political power to protect the unequal *status quo*. This experience of an abusive authority which hovered insistently over the political and civic expressions of life in Northern Ireland undoubtedly coloured my take on authority.

My irritation has also has something to do with the church of the 1960s which was attempting to escape from the ecclesiastical prison that had been created over the previous centuries. The church that existed pre-Vatican II was governed in a rigidly authoritarian manner where there was a definitive pecking order and the laity knew their place, which was effectively at the bottom of the heap, best captured by Pope Leo who spoke for a dominant clerical mindset when he unashamedly declared that the role of the laity was 'to pay, pray and obey'. The assumed authoritative position of the clerical caste in all matters of religious life and in many aspects of civic life created a claustrophobic environment which choked freedom of enquiry and freedom to imagine. One incident in my final year of secondary school brought this reality home to me forcibly.

I was studying A level English and had the joy to have a wonderful gem of an English teacher, a layman who was passionate, imaginative and absolutley inspiring. Under his tutelage, I began to devour books and, with his permission, I was allowed to choose a book to study by myself (on the syllabus but not being taught formally in class by him).

One day in the senior study hall in 1969 I was immersed in the book, reading and making notes when the priest monitor hovered over me, lifted the book, read the title, looked at me with undisguised contempt and promptly confiscated the novel. It was *Sons and Lovers* by D. H. Lawrence, then a formal part of the Northern Ireland English Literature A Level syllabus. Despite my vehement protestations and the full vent of my teenage ire, it was arbitrarily deemed unsuitable by this self appointed moral guardian. I was seventeen and I was raging. I fumed for weeks. I suppose I still do, some forty years later.

Notwithstanding his disapproval and the non return of the book to me, I managed to circumvent his authority, bought another copy, studied it clandestinely and duly wrote on the book in my A level exam with some degree of success. That experience of a priest censoring my legitimate study reinforced for me a negative approach to such invasive and ill informed authority. In the overall scheme of things it was a small incident, but it undoubtedly left its mark on my thinking.

Authority at home was more nuanced. At times it demanded an unquestioning obedience to my father and mother.

Attendance at Mass, for example, was a non negotiable. Dissent here was not allowed. Minor acts of disobedience were dealt with by a clip around the ears, a slap, or a verbal warning. More serious misdemeanours received a more sustained physical punishment or longer spells of incarceration. However, my mother and father were sparing in their meting out of such punishment and there was always the opportunity to speak your mind, always the right to be heard, always the opportunity for atonement and ready forgiveness. Underpinning everything, there was a deep and genuine love which enabled an enduring of the corrective times and sweetened the moments of guidance when their surefooted wisdom nurtured life choices.

My recollection of this is that your own authority was allowed to grow within you and rights and responsibilities pertaining to such growth was gradually afforded to you. As you grew older more weight was given to your opinion and you were encouraged to think for yourself about most things. Authority was firm, clear and yet in some way open to other possibilities. There were times of definitive No's, times of Maybe's and lots of Yes's. In retrospect, it was an enviroment that gave life, that allowed you to breathe, to challenge, to become yourself, to find your way.

In more global terms, the child of the 60s was characterised as being more rebellious because of the historical milieu that then prevailed. Post World War II there had been a palpable sense of relief from the survivors and, in the aftermath, there was much more freedom given to the offspring of the survivor generation. Freedom was a buzz word. Breaking out of sterotypes and staitjackets of all kinds became the norm. It found expression in love-ins and drop-outs, and it spawned a hippy generation that thumbed its nose at authority and went in search of its own meaning and its own misguided Holy Grail, seeking enlightenment in drugs and esoteric eastern religions. Hairstyles, colourful clothes, unconventional lifestyles and rock music became emblematic symbols of rebellion against a perception of authority that was restrictive, inflexible, irrelevant and staid.

All of that and so much more helped to shape the me who approaches the question of authority with more than a degree of scepticism and suspicion. My own subsequent life experiences as a father, teacher and at times leader of others in a host of situations has caused me to look critically at how my own authority was exercised. In my reflections I have precious moments of gladness and significant moments of regret. I believe my understanding and exercise of authority grew and changed as I myself developed and matured. Authority, both in administering it and receiving it, changed me, sometimes for the better, other times for the worse.

Authority has often been understood as a possession but in a sense it cannot be owned. Authority in a real sense can only be given by others. It comes out of relationship. The misguided priest who confiscated my book did not persuade me that he was right. In fact it strengthened my resentment of his authority and it irrevocably damaged our relationship. It made me ever more likely to rebel and challenge him when the opportunity presented itself. I also found a way to avoid his imposition of authority.

My gem of an English teacher who so inspired me to read had a real authority, the kind that called me to respond with the best that I could offer. It was an authority which emanated from himself, an authority that gave him a kind of 'calling power'. His was a light but infectious touch which made me glad to respond and my yes to him was unqualified and total.

CHAPTER 2

Authority in the Secular

We are all products of our society and few of us can escape the
anti-authority milieu of our time. We live in a culture that is
steeped in relativity, one that promotes the individual's right to
question all authority. Yet Christians are called to a different
measure of authority. In Hebrew the word for a measuring rod
is *quaneh* and it refers to a definitive measure that is not arbitrary
but precise. In the words of St Paul:

> For there is no authority except from God, and those that
> exist have been instituted by God. (Rom 13:1-4)

It is against this background of a divine measuring rod that
Christians have been debating and negotiating their relationship to the tangled worlds of politics, economics, culture and
church for nearly two millennia. The essential nature of that unavoidable entanglement, and the distinctive character of the
Christian's presence in 'the world,' came into focus early. As the
Letter to Diognetus, most likely written in the second century,
reminds us, Christians are always 'resident aliens'[1] in the world,
for while Christians honour just rulers, obey just laws, and con-
tribute to the common good of whatever society in which they
find themselves, a Christian's ultimate loyalty is given to a kingdom that is elsewhere. Christians believe that history can only

---

1. Letter to Diognetus cited in an article by Michael Brundell O. Carm in
Spirituality (March-April 1996), a publication of the Irish Dominicans.
'The difference between Christians and other people is not a question
of nationality, language or custom. Christians do not live apart ... and
while they live happily in their own countries, their behaviour is more
like that of resident aliens ... For them, any foreign country is home and
any home can be a foreign country ... they live their lives here below but
their citizenship is in the heavens. They obey the laws which are laid
down, but in private life transcend such laws. They show love to everyone and yet everyone will persecute them ...'

be read in its fullness in the light of faith in the Risen Christ, the Lord of history. And in that perspective, history is both the arena of God's action and the preparation room to our true home, the 'city of the living God' (Heb 12:22). Christians live in history in a distinctive way. We know that 'here is no abiding city, no lasting stay' and that reality utterly colours our perspective.

Modernity

Scholars divide western philosophy into four major eras, ancient (up to Augustine 354-430), medieval (up to Descartes, 1596-1650), the modern (up to mid twentieth century) and the postmodern that is the current reality. The core rationale of modernity is that human reason should have the final say in how we structure our community and it should be the ultimate authority on how we govern all public life. Human reason is lauded and established as the final arbiter. Modernity, in essence, refuses to see in man any sort of transparent aspiration. It is the refusal of any sort of faith. It rejects mystery. From a Christian perspective, it is akin to a sort of Gnostic spirituality in that it seeks to substitute itself for the truths of Catholicism. It proposes that only doctrines acceptable to the norms of a given time can be believed. It seeks to fashion the church to the current acceptable scientific or cultural mores of the time. It refuses to recognise 'the democracy of the dead', a phrase attributed to G. K. Chesterton which he used to justify the church's tradition of examining the tenets of faith and morals within the total context of the tradition of the church, including those communities of faith that have preceded us.[2] Chesterton would be an expected advocate for the church's opposition to the heresy of modernity, but a much more unlikely

2. It comes from Chesterton's book, *Orthodoxy*, Chapter 4, 'The Ethics of Elfland.' It actually reads: 'Tradition means giving a vote to the most obscure of all classes, our ancestors. It is the democracy of the dead.' Chesterton goes on to say: 'Tradition refuses to submit to the small and arrogant oligarchy of those who merely happen to be walking about. All democrats object to men being disqualified by the accident of birth; tradition objects to their being disqualified by the accident of death. Democracy tells us not to neglect a good man's opinion, even if he is our groom; tradition asks us not to neglect a good man's opinion, even if he is our father.'

supporter against the grandiose claims of modernity is Albert Camus.

In one of his essays, 'Helen's Exile' that appeared in *Cahiers du Sud* [3] Helen has come to represent for Camus the Greek sense of reason, a reason that was limited, not infinite, as modernity would have us believe. Camus argues:

> History explains neither the natural universe which came before it, nor beauty which stands above it. Consequently, it has chosen to ignore them. Whereas Plato incorporated everything – nonsense, reason, and myth – our philosophers admit nothing but nonsense or reason. The mole is meditating. It was Christianity that began to replace the contemplation of the world with the tragedy of the soul. [4]

In commenting on this passage, James Schall speaks of those spectres that cannot be accounted for by pure intellect: 'they were forced to go under ground. They did not disappear but could be found still rooting about the human condition like an annoying mole disturbing the smooth surface of our own carefully planned gardens in which we allow planted only what we want there. We alone, we think, are the movers and the shakers, the planters and the planted. But the mole continues to disturb our rationalist schools.' [5]

In an interview for the Italian journal, *Trenta Giorni*, Henri Cardinal de Lubac characterises modernity as 'the refusal to see in man any sort of transcendent aspiration … it is the refusal of any sort of faith. It follows on the rejection of mystery. Modernity will always 'know' more, will always 'explain' more, but in reality it will not 'comprehend' more, because it has refused mystery.' [6] Ultimately, Modernism is a representation of the old Pelagian heresy that we can redeem ourselves.

Yet the dominant imprint of modernism remains steadfastly embedded in our cultures. It is characterised most by a secularist mentality, one that lauds the here and now, the get and have

---

3. Abert Camus, *Lyrical and Critical Essays*, trs Ellen Conroy Kennedy (New York: Vintage, 1968), 148-153.
4. Ibid.
5. James V. Schall, *Does Catholicism Still Exist?* (New York: Alba House, 1994), 137.
6. *Trenta Giorni* 3 (1985) p 10.

mindset, the cult of the individual, the exiling of religious sensibility to a private cult, the self-authority of man as the only true *quaneh* or measure. Man is not judged by Truth. He alone is the ultimate judge of truth.

Secularism

In Ireland in 2006 at the Humbert Summer School in Co Mayo, Archbishop Diarmuid Martin delivered a provocative speech on secularism. He contended that although Ireland had been invaded in the past by invading armies today its most dangerous invader was a cultural force, a modernist spirit, one of whose armies was secularism.

Secularity is a term coined around 1850 'to denote a system which sought to order and interpret life on principles taken solely from this world, without recourse to belief in God and a future world'.[7] Secularity has its origins in this era of modernity whose founding father was René Descartes. Descartes' radical theory was a *volte-face* to what had gone before. The ancient and medieval eras had largely accepted that divine authority, not human rationality, was the supreme authority. Where once prefaces such as 'God says', 'the church says', 'the king says' would have been normative, today it is more likely to be 'reason says', 'democracy says'. Secularity believes this latter way of thinking is the ultimate authority. However, even within secularity there is a wide gamut of expressions ranging from outright hostility towards the religious mindset to a positive inclusive relationship that sees religion as a major contributor to peace and harmony in our world.

Bad Press

Perhaps the church has been too absolute and narrow in its analysis. Perhaps in the past the churches have been too ready to condemn secularism because it challenged their worldview and the churches saw it as the enemy of spirituality. It was too easy to caricature secularism as the antithesis of religion. Undoubtedly, secularism in its most rampant and aggressive form can be in-

---

7. Ronald Rolheiser, *Secularity and the Gospel* (Crossroad Publishing Company, 2006) 39.

imical to the fostering of faith and its value but it is important to remember that while it demands 'freedom from religion it also mandates freedom for religion'.[8]

It could be argued, notwithstanding obvious exceptions, that secular culture contains much of what is best in the Judaeo-Christian tradition. We could cite human dignity, equality of race and gender, equal opportunity for all, tolerance, peace making, fairness, hospitality, justice, openness to the transcendent etc. Of course, there are aberrations but no culture can be judged solely on these. We judge cultures on what is most noble within them, not on what is most deviant.[9]

On the other hand it would be naïve not to acknowledge that there is a danger in the extreme secular position whereby truth becomes relative to the individual and one is caught up into a selfishness that merely feeds the ego. This can result in economic structures that benefit the rich to the detriment of the poor, in sexual irresponsibility, in a devaluation of family, in drug abuse, in pornography, in euthanasia and in a general disrespect for life.

The main thrust of this cursory overview of secularism is to suggest that it needs a better press in church circles. Yes, it has deficits and dangers, but it also has graces and strengths. Somewhat like the church itself, it can be a 'chaste harlot' (St Augustine), both saint and sinner. It cannot be dismissed simply as an ogre or as public enemy number one. It is in this secular world that the church has to learn to dialogue. It has to learn to speak the language of the people. It cannot operate out of a medieval or ancient paradigm of authority because no one is listening to such a voice. It can only speak out of solidarity with its people who live and move and think and act in the midst of a secular reality. The church voice and its exercise of authority can only be effective if it leads its people from where they are, concretely, in their everyday reality. It must call them to a divine perspective but it does so from the concrete lives of the people. This demands a commitment to move away from monologue to a genuine dialogue as articulated so wonderfully by John XXIII in his opening speech of the Second Vatican Council.

8. Ibid., 41.
9. Ibid., 42.

The Civic Forum

Within the civic forum, we now live in a democracy, however flawed, and the political authority figures who present themselves in various positions have to be mandated. The fact that they have been fairly elected helps their relationship with the general populace and this dynamic creates an environment of mutual dependency. We need them to be effective in order to govern and exercise authority, they need us to be sure of returning to their position. Undue abuse of their authority will wreak its own whirlwind.

Even within positions of civic responsibility such as tax offices, hospitals, schools etc., increasingly there are codes of conduct whereby those who exercise authority are themselves governed by codes of ethics and there are expectations as to how they are to meet and deal with the public. In Ireland in 2005 we witnessed uproar when it was discovered that some solicitors were overcharging victims who had applied to the Redress Board for compensation. The abuse of their authoritative position forced the Law Society to remedy this ill and to take punitive action where misdemeanours had occurred

In civilian life we have a plethora of examples where authority is acountable. One only has to look at the advent of ombudsmen and women whose task is to oversee the exercise of authority by various state agencies and departments. In Northern Ireland, the creation of the Police Ombudsman created a whole new dynamic to protect against the abuse of authority. The Fair Employment Agency was another example of attempts to curtail the abuse of privilege afforded to the Protestant community and to create a level playing pitch for Catholics.

Static Authority of Church

All of these developments stand in sharp contrast to progress in the church, which has largely remained quite static in its structures and exercise of authority. In the eyes of many critics, both inside and outside of the church, significant authority is wielded by an unelected minority and most of the church is effectively disenfranchised. The officeholders are not accountable to the rank and file membership who have little say in how the church is managed or how its resources are used. This remains the situation forty years after Vatican II which held out the promise of the People of God taking up their rightful duties and responsibilities, not as some privilege accorded to them, but as an inalienable right of their baptism. This distribution of power and effective decision making within the hands of a small cohort of the faithful prevents a real sense of engagement and belonging, and is one significant factor in the laity's abdication of its responsibility for the welfare of the church and ther spread of the gospel. 'Believing but not belonging' (Grace Davies) has become normative for many of the baptised. Part of the problem is in the centralisation of authority and the effective ignoring of the voice of the body. Part of the solution will be to rectify this aberration.

Some would argue that, in the secular realm, the province of government is a natural one, over which man has dominion because men and women who are human persons like ourselves govern us. It is therefore in keeping with our dignity that we should participate in some way in ordering secular affairs. They would proceed to argue that with the church the province is the supernatural order, over which we have no dominion. Jesus Christ who shares our nature governs the church, but this sharing does not exhaust his personhood. In simple terms, Christ is a superior being; therefore, it is precisely in keeping with the dignity of our nature that we recognise that superiority and permit him to govern in the church. These advocates would acknowledge the uncomfortable fact that Christ governs through his vicar, the pope, a mere man; that this man guides a hierarchy of purely human agents; and that there are precious few guarantees against the inadequacy of all that is human in the church. But despite these drawbacks, they would hold that the essential identity, purpose and domain of the church would be lost if she were governed in any other way.

Faithful Catholics are all too aware that the church is not and cannot be a democracy, but equally the church is not meant to be a monarchy or an oligarchy and, too often while decrying those who call for more democratic elements, the church ignores the regal trappings it has accrued over the centuries. It must be recognised that the dominant culture esteems freedom *from* more than freedom *for*. The church is called to be the best that she can be, both human and divine, and this should not therefore exclude democratic elements that could only enrich the life of the church. The divine life of the church is guaranteed because the Lord has promised to be with us always even to the ends of time and we know that the gates of hell will not prevail against it. However, the human element is always suspect, with the possibility of greatness and baseness present in each of us.

In 1966, shortly after the Second Vatican Council, William D'Antonio, one of the authors of a new book on the rise of the laity in the church, predicted that in the long run laypersons would do what seems rational and practical whenever a church tradition could not be sustained by what they saw as sound reasons.[10] These surveys indicated that his prediction was remarkably accurate. There is clearly a gradual move from conformity to autonomy among Catholics.

In 1987 and again in 1993 D'Antonio and others constructed a questionnaire and commissioned the Gallup organisation to sample some 800 American Roman Catholics 18 years old and older. Both samples had error margins of [+ or -] 4 per cent. The responses, of course, do not present us with a clear picture of what would constitute acceptable behaviour for a Catholic today on important social/moral issues. But a majority of Catholics were prepared to allow that those practising contraceptive birth control, attending Mass less than weekly, ignoring the pope's annual campaign for funds, and divorcing/remarrying may still be good Catholics. Even those most highly committed to the institutional church gave significant support to this new image.

Respondents were asked who should have the moral authority to decide what was right or wrong in five specific areas of social conduct, all having to do with sexual behaviour and marriage. The options were: church leaders, individuals making up their own minds, or individuals and church leaders working together to define and determine what was moral. In both polls respondants rejected the moral authority of the church leaders acting alone. By more than a two to one margjn, they declared that individuals alone or acting with church leaders should decide

10. William V. D'Antonio, James D. Davidson, Dean R. Hoge and Katherine Meyer, *American Catholics: Gender, Generation, and Commitment*, (AltaMira Press, 2001).

the morality of these behaviours. In none of the five items do more than one in four Catholics say that moral authority should reside with church leaders alone. Given the effort by church leaders during the past five years to make abortion a litmus test for Catholic orthodoxy, insisting that the topic was not open for discussion, the laity's response is disturbing. Equally striking is the laity's sense of social responsibility, manifested in their desire to share decision-making power with the hierarchy, for that was the dominant shift in responses between 1987 and 1993.

Trend data from two Gallup polls taken in 1987 and again in 1993 show that there has emerged within the American Catholic laity a pattern of attitudes, beliefs and behaviours about Roman Catholicism and being a Roman Catholic that are at variance with the traditional attitudes, beliefs and behaviours sanctioned by the Vatican. These patterns lend strong support to the contention that they constitute a form of pluralism within the church. The legitimacy of the teaching authority of the Vatican, as manifested in particular by the pope, has been called into question on a range of moral issues involving especially marriage and sexual conduct. Beyond that, the laity want more democracy in parish, diocesan and even Vatican affairs.[11]

This research shows that Catholics have high levels of support for the basic dogmas (sacraments, the Resurrection and the Real Presence in the Eucharist, for example), but that they are more likely to reach their own conclusions in areas where non-theologians and non-clerics have some expertise (sexual issues, capital punishment and church governance, for example).

The laity have come to understand that all organisations run by human beings are subject to revision over time and that participatory forms of governance are useful for safeguarding against abusive relationships, especially in hierarchical systems which can sometimes be unmindful of human rights.

The call for active participation by the church in public affairs is not new. Early in the last century, Cardinal Jozef Cardijn of Belgium used the slogan 'Observe, Judge and Act' in found-

---

11. see, D'Anlonio, W. V., 1992, 'Autonomy and Community: Indicators of Change Among the American Catholic Laity', pp 1-23 in *Proceedings of the Fifty-fourth Annual Convention, Canon Law Society of America,* Washington, DC: Catholic University of America Press.

ing Young Christian Workers and Young Christian Students. From these initially European groups, the idea spread into the labour movement and Christian Family Movement in the United States. Prior to that, Pope Leo XIII had called for Catholic action in public affairs.

Since the sad disclosures about sex abuse in the church in Boston and elsewhere, participating in church governance by the laity has increased, particularly in the American church. For example, Voice of the Faithful, a lay organisation which seeks, among other things, to shape structural changes within the church, has grown rapidly since its founding in Boston in the spring of 2002. A commensurate engagement by laity in the Irish church has not yet occurred.

Hierarchy as Charism

Catholics hold that the hierarchy is a singular charism given to the church, especially to the bishop who has been entrusted with 'the sure charism of truth'. However, as with all charisms, this too can fade and die unless it is nurtured and revitalised. Even a cursory look at the tradition and evolution of authority within our church clearly reveals that it has evolved. Not all structures are written in stone. To query the why of something is not to be disrespectful. Children pose the question interminably as most parents know. To also ask 'Why not? 'is equally valid and it is out of such engagements that truth finds its voice. To avoid the debate or to take refuge in stock answers that do not speak authentically to the reality of people's lived experience is unworthy of all leaders who seek to emulate the one who came 'to serve not to be served'.

Gregorian Reforms of the 11th Century

Church structure has moved a long way from the church of Gregory the Great who in many ways was the architect of the current hierarchical structure. It was because of the eleventh-century reforms of Gregory VII that the church increasingly took on a specific figure, the 'Gregorian form' which institutionalised 'hierarchy' as a principle. No longer were order and structure only necessary for the church, they became 'constitutive' of the church. As Gaillardetz put it, 'What Gregory set in motion was a gradual but inexorable shift from a church whose foundation lay in theology and sacramental practice to a church whose foundation lay in canon law.'[12] A European theologian, Ghislan Lafont shows how this mentality can be seen in the Catholic Church's repeated refrain regarding the 'hierarchical constitution of the church' in its documents from the last hundred years – not wrong, as far as it goes, but not central or primary either.[13] Thus, when the Neoplatonic, Pseudo-Dionysian thought permeated ecclesiology under Pope Gregory VII and his successors, hierarchy became synonymous with the clergy.

According to Pseudo-Dionysius, truth and value are communicated in a downward movement from above: higher beings communicate reality to lower beings and thereby act as mediators of truth and value which would not come to lower beings without this mediation from above. When the clergy are thought of in this way, they become the depositories of truth and grace. And even here, in the clerical order, the distinction between higher and lower obtains: the pope communicates to those below him, the bishops, who communicate truth to priests. Finally, priests communicate to the religious, who communicate truth to the laity. On these assumptions, the pope is higher than the bishops, bishops are higher than priests, priests are higher than vowed religious, religious are higher than married persons. Truth and holiness always come from mediators who are above in the chain of hierarchies. Nothing, by the way, can go in the inverse direction, so that the clergy cannot learn anything from the religious or the laity. Such an exaggerated emphasis on the dichotomies within Pseudo-Dionysius' understanding of hierarchy created imbalances, discontinuities, and ruptures in the church's understanding of authority, ministry, and the basic dignity of every baptised person. By the same token, such an understanding of hierarchy meant that the 'church' was superior to the 'world,' the pope to the secular prince.

12. See Richard Gaillardetz, *The Church in the Making* (Mahwah, NJ: Paulist Press, 2006) 41.
13. Ghislain Lafont, *Imaginer l'Église Catholique* (Paris, Editions du Cerf, 1995).

Application to Revelation

Lafont proceeds to examine how this theory of hierarchy is worked out when applied to the areas of revealed truth. Revelation is no longer a matter of the whole church, the community of believers, but the province of its clerical leaders. The faithful, lay and vowed religious, learn revealed truth from their priests, whose understanding is regulated by the bishops' higher perception of truth. In turn, bishops must obey the teachings of the pope, himself the recipient of divine truth from Christ, whose Vicar he is. Arriving at religious truth is not a matter of adverting to one's experience, sharing and clarifying it, not a matter of personal study or prayerful consideration, not an affair of testing and validating, but of listening to and obeying the church's authoritative teachers, who cannot be mistaken because they are protected from error by Christ's Spirit of truth. The principle of mediation is clear and determined: the Christian always looks to the person or office that is immediately higher. The whole structure of the 'hierarchical church' rests on this principle.

Analysis

Whereas 'hierarchy' emerged from Neoplatonic thought as represented in Pseudo-Dionysius in particular, 'modernity' emerged from European Enlightenment efforts which were bound up with the primacy of the individual subject, the superiority of reason over physical matter, the autonomy of freedom over society's traditions and heteronomy, and the dichotomy between object and subject making valid knowledge possible. The church rejected 'modernity' and Western intelligentsia rejected 'hierarchy.' The church in particular came to understand itself as fully independent of society, not interactive and a part of the world but 'other than the world' and superior to it. It had its own 'body,' the ecclesial one, and no longer constituted the larger, cosmic body of Christ. Like the state, it, too, was a 'perfect society.' The ramifications of such a separation have proven harmful not only to the church but to the world as well.

Higher Calling

My late mother used to speak of the role of the clergy and religious life in terms of people who had received a 'higher calling'. She was a product of her time and it was the dominant culture of that era which accorded such an accolade to religious personnel. It was and is a flawed theology, one which did a great disservice not only to the ultimate dignity of all the baptised but thwarted the emegence of an authentic lay voice and elevated the cleric and religious to an impossible pedestal of perfection.

The church, however, has attempted to change because it knows that it is a living reality moving within the context of history towards its final goal which is the kingdom of the Father. In the Second Vatican Council it reaffirmed the true dignity of baptism which makes us all equally the sons and daughters of the Father. Moreover, it also articulated its desire 'to not only address the sons of the church, and all who call upon the name of Christ, but the whole of humanity as well, and it longs to set forth the way it understands the presence and the function of the church in the world today.'[14] To take up that challenge it needs to look again at how authority is exercised.

---

14. *Gaudium et Spes*, par 2.

CHAPTER 3

The Vexed Question of Subsidiarity

The stubborn lingering of the Pseudo-Dionysius reforms of Gregory VII has done much to thwart the genuine acceptance and integration of the principle of subsidiarity within church structures. Although it was first given formal magisterial approval in Pius XI's 1931 encyclical, *Quadragesimo Anno*, it could be argued that its vision reaches back to medieval Christian experience, albeit in less focused terms. Pope Pius XII extended the sphere of application when he commented in 1946 that this principle, 'valid for social life in all its grades' was valid 'also for the life of the church without prejudice to its hierarchical structure.'[1] Sharper definitions were later to be developed by Pope John XXIII and by the Second Vatican Council and the subject received particular attention from Pope John Paul II in *Centesimus Annus*.

At its core, it maintains that a society flourishes best when its citizens recognise that different social organisations have different tasks. The subsidiarity principle, valid for both the secular and the ecclesiastical realm, demands that those in authority recognise the rights of the different members of society. It calls upon those in higher authority to respect the rights of those in lower authority. Families, friends, associates, churches, local charitable organisations – these should be the first to respond to the needs of their brothers and sisters. Government should only be directly involved as the organisation of last resort and should implement policies designed to support rather than replace intermediary groups. In this way, people are induced to serve one another, as Christ commanded. In effect, this means that in family life, matters should be left to that domestic unit as much as

---

1. Pope Pius XII made this statement in a talk to newly created cardinals, *AAS* 38 (1946), 144-5.

possible and where support is needed it should be provided by the lowest level of government possible.

Irony

There is a certain irony that the church, which has been such a protagonist for the subsidiarity viewpoint within secular society, seems to ignore this perspective when it comes to church governance and behaviour. Rightly, it argues that there should be limits on state power and interventions in private affairs and it cautions against certain aspects of 'the welfare state' which can easily arrogate to central authorities activities that are properly the function of more intermediary institutions or the family itself.

One school of thought would contend that from the beginning of its existence, Catholicism has been confronted by the idolatry of the state. History is sadly full of tragic incidents where the state assumed powers that led to excessive and unwarranted intrusion and control over individuals and society. The twentieth century spawned Facism, Nazism and Communism, all of which damaged the fabric of the societies they infected. Yet it is not a one sided story. History is also full of incidents where the church interfered with and damaged the lives of individuals and societies. One could cite the Inquisition, the Crusades and the Syllabus of Errors as well as the more recent and notoriously inept handling of the child sex abuse scandals.Within the Irish context, we have in recent memory the powerful veto that the church held over much of civic life until the last decades of the twentieth century.

As well as being the villain, at times, the state has also been instrumental in a positive way in controlling the excesses of the church. The religious wars within Europe that pitted Catholics and Protestants against each other were only resolved by the intervention of the state and the growth of what has become known as *laïcité*. Many a representation of the French Revolution and of the separation between church and state associates *laïcité* with a negative anti-clerical, anti-religion political strategy. Philippe Portier calls it the *laïcité primitive*.[2] He argues

---

2. See Philippe Portier, 'De la séparation à la reconnaissance. L'évolu-

that *laïcité* is to be situated at the heart of the development of Christianity. In the 16th and 17th centuries the secular civil authorities instituted themselves in order to achieve a juridical policy of pacification among Catholics and Protestants.[3] *Laïcité* was the result of political wisdom, of a subtle sense of balance, which doesn't force anybody to give up personal convictions, but rather introduces a new art of living together.[4] *Laïcité* represents a double memory: the history of a legal process of putting things into a new civic order, and the history of a social process of secularisation. Institutions are separated and secularised, but the religious cults are respected as regards their proper and specific aims. As Charles de Gaulle put it, the state is secular, but France is Christian. Today the positive side of this can be seen in France where often the church and state engage in mutually beneficial and respectful dialogue with each other.

Yet the church too has been a voice for the powerless and a strong advocate of freedom for those under the yoke of oppressive state governments and regimes. She has developed and advocated the principle of subsidiarity, according to which 'a community of a higher order should not interfere in the internal life of a lower order, depriving the latter of its functions, but rather should support it in case of need and help to co-ordinate its activity with the activities of the rest of society, always with a view to the common good.'[5] In essence this view argues that as many things as possible should be left to individuals and voluntary organisations. Behind this concept is the more basic notion that individuals have internal resources and are themselves the origins and purposes of all action, even of action attributed to the state.

---

tion du regime Francais de laïcité,' in Armogathe, Jean-Robert, Williame, Jean-Paul, Portier, Philippe, Fondation Singer-Polignac Paris, *Les mutations contemporaines du religieux*, (Bibliothèque de L'école des hautes études. Sciences réligieuses 119, Brepols,Turnhout, 2003),1-24, 5.
3. See The Edict of Nantes (1598), the 'religious peace' of Augsburg (1555), the Treaty of Westphalia (1648).
4. Emile Poulat, *Notre laïcité publique. 'La France est une Republique laïque'* (*Constitutions de 1946 et 1958*), (Paris, Berg International, 2003) 13.
5. *Centesimus Annus*, 48.

Semper Reformanda

Seeking greater autonomy for individual bishops and local churches, Catholic reformers frequently invoke the principle of subsidiarity, arguing that it needs to be more sensitive to this issue within its own governmental structures. Obviously, the ancient principle of subsidiarity, which demands that higher authority not intervene in the operation of smaller units unless they are unable to attend to their own needs, favours de-centralisation. From studying antiquity we can see clearly that the Catholic Church respected this principle. However, since the centralisation of the church in the papacy, the principle of subsidiarity has not been adequately applied, nor has it been a significant topic of reflection in official ecclesiologies.

Recent church teaching, especially through John Paul II, has emphasised that people are meant to be subjects, not objects, in the social organisations to which they belong. Workers are to be subjects, not objects, of the productive process. People are meant to participate in the important organisational decisions that affect their lives.

Recognising this as a deficit in the church, Francis A. Sullivan SJ maintains that 'there is an urgent need for changes that would provide for a more effective participation of priests, members of religious orders, and lay men and women in the processes by which decisions are made in our church.' Sullivan suggests opening up plenary councils, none of which has been held in the US since 1884, to a wider participation of the groups named above, plus presidents of Catholic universities, seminary rectors, and ecumenical 'guests'. (These comments could be applicable throughout the worldwide church.) Sullivan would change canon law to give all those who have a consultative vote (this excludes the 'guests') the right to propose matter for the agenda and 'a deliberate vote in deciding which questions are to be treated by the synod'.[6] Sullivan also suggests changes in the law regarding diocesan synods, obliging bishops to hold a diocesan council whenever two-thirds of both the presbyteral council and the diocesan pastoral council judge that circumstances warrant it. Even though these tentative suggestions deal solely with the

6. See 'The Authority of the Diocesan Bishop in the Roman Catholic Church' in *Lutheran Forum* 37, No 1, 2003, 34-35.

local church, they could have implications for the universal church as well.

Congregation for Divine Worship

It is a sad reality that organs of the church sometimes thwart the principles of subsidiarity. A current example that received much media attention is the way that the Congregation for Divine Worship and the Sacraments has dealt with the International Commission for English in the Liturgy, a body set up by the Conferences of English-speaking bishops around the world. It has *de facto* rejected its proposals for inclusive language, restructured the Commission itself, and scrapped new texts proposed by the Commission.

The Head of the Congregation, Cardinal Medina Estevez, refused to accept the agreed revised translation of the Sacramentary as submitted by the English-speaking bishops from different regions. All this bypasses the principle of subsidiarity, which holds that a higher authority should not interfere in or decide matters that are within the competence of lesser authorities, and should also give them active support. Canon 833 clearly states, 'It pertains to Episcopal Conferences to prepare translations', but the current practice suggests that the Roman Curia have gone beyond this literal meaning of the canon and have reserved to themselves the right to prepare the texts.[7] Preparation of the English translation was an international effort involving all of the Conferences of Bishops, where English is the main language, and the processes used embodied both collegiality and communion. Refusal of permission to publish, when the majority of Bishops had accepted the text was a serious blow to the concepts of communion and collegiality in the Catholic Church. It seems that the Congregation went beyond its competence, since approval to publish is not required by the canons. The action of the Congregation reinforced centralising tendencies that seem to be opposed to the intention of the Council. Apart from the fact that the Conference has the right to prepare translations, it seems that the intention of the canon 838 is to recognise two critical aspects of communion, namely subsidiarity and inculturation.

7. Canon Law Society, 'Trust The Code of Canon Law', Collins Liturgical Publications (in English translation 1983), 139.

The local community seems best suited to prepare translations that reflect both the best language usage appropriate to the Latin original and to make necessary adaptations to the culture of the local people. More importantly, what does the practice of communion have to say about the reality of the theory? To restore unity and communion no burden must be imposed beyond what is strictly necessary (Decree on Ecumenism, *Unitatis redintegratio* n 18; cf Acts 15:28).

Leadership within communion does not dominate. It respects the principle of unity in diversity and the principle of subsidiarity, which is not the same thing as delegation. It affirms the autonomy of each particular church. 'Without autonomy there can only be the master-slave relationship.'[8] Autonomy is not independence, but the right of a particular church to live the gospel and organise its life and liturgy in keeping with the particular culture and genius of its people, and in harmony with the other churches of the same regional communion. The exercise of vigilance in the matter of oversight at the universal, regional and local levels requires knowledge, understanding, consultation and trust, if true communion is to be maintained, enhanced and restored.

Generally speaking, the pope's oversight is meant to be exercised in collaboration with the leaders of other churches and the other members of the episcopal college. Only in close communion with them can the Bishop of Rome acquire the necessary knowledge and wisdom to respect the truth of the maxim cited in the Vatican II document *Gaudium et spes, The Church in the Modern World: 'In necessariis unitas, in dubiis libertas, in omnibus caritas.'* (In necessary matters let there be unity, in matters unsettled let there be freedom, and in all things let there be charity.)[9]

Subsidiarity within ecclesial structures is often lacking. That Christians are to be subjects in the church, and hence co-responsible for the important ecclesiastical decisions, has not been taken seriously in the official Catholic ecclesiologies. The recent emphasis of Roman Catholic social teaching on human rights and civil liberties has not given rise to serious reflection of what

8. See John Linnan, 'Theology and Renewing the Structure of the Petrine Office', *New Theology Review* 13:3 (August 2000), 40.
9. Vatican II, 'The Church in the Modern World', *Gaudium et spes*, # 92.

this means for Catholics in the Catholic Church. Leonard Boff found himself in difficulty over his views on this issue in a 1986 publication.[10] It was raised as an important issue in the 1985 Synod of Bishops, which proposed a study of the applicability of the principle of subsidiarity to the internal life of the church. The most benign interpretation of its fate since that time is that of Dulles who suggests that it is being allowed 'to mature in theological literature before the magisterium makes a formal pronouncement.'[11]

As Avery Dulles pointed out in this article which appeared in the America magazine,[12] the principle of subsidiarity was first articulated in relation to secular governments which are established from below. Given that the church is established from above, there is significant debate and no little degree of uncertainty as to how this principle applies within the church. It is an unsettling insertion into church structures because it calls for *communio* not only in words but also in deeds. Each section of the church should be allowed to exercise a legitimate freedom whereby decisions taken by those sections need to be referred to church leaders who have a wider responsibility. Both a strong teaching office that recognises the need for building consensus, and a de-centralised form of church governance, are required in order to maintain unity and strengthen the bonds of communion. Put negatively, if the jurisdictional authority of the Bishop of Rome insinuates itself into the life of local churches in an unwarranted manner, and if the pastoral authority of local bishops in their own churches is not respected, then communion becomes defective.

---

10. Leonardo Boff, *Church: Charism and Power – LiberationTheology and the Institutional Church* (New York: Crossroad), 1985.
11. Avery Dulles,'The Papacy for a Globalized Church', *America*, vol 183 (July 15th 2000).
12. Ibid.

CHAPTER 4

Church and Papacy

The biblical and patristic studies movements that were embraced by Catholic scholars in the early twentieth century assisted the church to recover older images of itself, like the rediscovery of a trunk full of old photographs in a grandparents' house can renew interest in old images of the family and rekindle stories from the family tradition.[1]

It's a lovely image, rooting around in the family photograph album and being sparked to recollect and discover something of our tradition and heritage which we might have forgotten or even lost forever. Perhaps as a result of his own delving into the traditions of the church, the late Pope John Paul II was prompted to initiate an unusual exercise.

In May 1995, John Paul II issued a remarkable encyclical letter on ecumenism, *Ut Unum Sint* ('That They May Be One'). It was a surprising document not only for its reflective and prayerful style but also for its provocative content. One of its most startling proposals was an invitation to the church to think together about ways for the papacy to become a more authentic symbol of unity rather than division. The pope acknowledged that for many today it is a divisive position and, without renouncing any of the long held traditions and beliefs that underpin the validity of the papacy, he invited the church to discern how best for the role to be exercised in the name of unity.

He spoke of the need 'to find a way of exercising the primacy which, while in no way renouncing what is essential to its mission, is nonetheless open to a new situation' (n. 95). He invited Christian leaders and theologians to engage with him 'in a patient

---

1. Anthony Gooley, 'Has the Catholic Church lost its way with the revival of genuine Episcopal collegiality?' found at http://dlibrary. acu.edu.au/research/theology/ejournal/aet_1/Gooley.htm

and fraternal dialogue on this subject, a dialogue in which, leaving useless controversies behind, we could listen to one another, keeping before us only the will of Christ for his church' (n. 96). It was a bold and somewhat shocking request because it recognised that new situations require new methodologies and perhaps new structures. New wine and old wineskins come to mind.

Some of the early responses from other Christian churches seemed to say that the very existence of the primacy as it had been defined at Vatican I and Vatican II was ecumenically unacceptable. But more recently the Anglican/Roman Catholic International Commission indicated a remarkable openness on the part of Anglicans to the idea of a universal papal primacy[2] and individual Protestant theologians such as Wolfhart Pannenberg have seen the desirability of having a pope for all Christians.[3]

Also, if as *Ut Unum Sint* maintains, 'complementary formulations of dogmatic truth prove that the content of the faith can truly speak to all cultures,' and that according to John Paul II, 'the expression of truth can take different forms,' the ways in which the pope determines and publicly states that truth would seem to require, at the very least, extensive consultation. First, there is the matter of internal consultation with a broad spectrum of the Catholic Church, which could be carried out more extensively. Secondly, there is the matter of regular and ongoing ecumenical consultation that could be conducted more comprehensively. Third, to what extent can the pope exercise and assert his teaching authority, not just to Catholics, but to separated brothers and sisters in the faith?

Creating a clear break with the distinctly pyramidal structure applied to the church from the Middle Ages, collegiality runs right through the Vatican II documents. Dulles sees a broad meaning here, as part of the 'spirit' of Vatican II. 'Thus the principle of collegiality ... may be understood as pervading all levels

---

2. See *Origins*, 5/27/99.

3. *A Pope for All Christians? An Inquiry Into the Role of Peter in the Modern Church*, ed. Peter J. McCord (New York: Paulist, 1976), with contributions by distinguished theologians representing the Lutheran, Roman Catholic, Baptist, Reformed, Orthodox, Methodist and Anglican perspectives.

of the church.'[4] Dulles sees collegiality as impacting on decision-making right through to how the whole church, laity included, shares responsibility. The challenge of collegiality is the construction of decision-making structures that respect the tradition of hierarchy and the nature of the church as a Spirit-filled (and therefore wisdom-filled) community of people

As Paul Collins puts it:

We need popes who are servants, like Jesus himself, not lords of the world, as some of the mediaeval popes thought they were. We need popes who see themselves as a focus for the church's unity, not the sole theological oracles, legal owners and administrators of the ecclesial institution. We need a new way of modelling the papacy for a new cultural and ecclesiastical situation.[5]

Crisis

Authority is perhaps the single greatest issue that confronts the Catholic Church today. The issue of who legitimately protects the faith, interprets the tradition, and controls the internal decision-making of the church is a perennial one but there is a feeling that this seemingly perennial 'crisis of authority' has reached its historic highpoint in the post-Vatican II Catholic Church.

As Aquinas pointed out, theology, in seeking to be a language about God and all things in relation to God, has a unique starting point and conclusion. It presupposes the God of Jesus Christ as the ultimate reference point. Therefore any examination of church and governance is judged by the authority of God as witnessed in the life of his son, Jesus Christ. The Catholic Church is, unashamedly, hierarchical although *Lumen Gentium* significantly altered our perception of what that really means.

Pre-Vatican II the structure was one of an episcopal hierarchy and clergy with an attached people.Today, through the teachings of *Lumen Gentium* and other conciliar documents, it is understood as a whole people of God with a hierarchical structure internal to itself. Unfortunately, the reality of this new

4. See Avery Dulles, 'Vatican II Reform: The Basic Principles', *Church* (Summer 1985): 7
5. Paul Collins, *Upon This Rock: The Popes and Their Changing Role* (Melbourne: Melbourne University Press, 2000) viii.

understanding is very slow in taking root. Some of the reasons for this would include an ill informed education of the church membership and a stubborn clinging to the ancient model by those who operate out of the older theological paradigm. Authority within the Catholic Church is largely exercised through an hierarchical structure with the pope seen as the boss or the one with the final say. There is a tendency to assume that the way the papacy operates today is the way it has always been. We have become used to the practice of the pope appointing bishops or issuing encylicals or decrees that have an authoritative voice in most of the Catholic world. But it was not ever thus. There has been an ongoing evolution in the role and authority of the pope, one which owes its current *modus operandi* more to history and circumstance than any scriptural or patristic basis.

Papal Election

In 2005 we had the election of a new pope. It is important to stress that the papal election is not a sacrament. One is not ordained pope. One becomes pope because one is the first bishop of the local church of Rome which acquired from ancient times a distinctive primacy among all the churches. With the demise of the church of Jerusalem near the end of the first century, Rome became the centre, largely due to the tradition that it received the apostolic tradition from two apostles, Sts Peter and Paul. It is worth recalling the remark of Cardinal Suenens: 'A pope's finest moment is not that of his election or consecration, but that of his baptism.'[6]

Some 112 cardinals spent a number of days in prayer and dicussion and elected Cardinal Ratzinger who adopted the title Benedict XVI. He is the new leader of the 1.2 billion Catholics worldwide. I have no doubt that the new pope is a good and holy man, one who comes with a deserved reputation as a superb theologian. I have no doubt also that men who exercised their votes were men of prayer and their decision was influenced considerably by this dimension and by their concerns for the spiritual welfare of the church and the world. However, it would be naïve to think that the election is not also a political process.

6. Quoted in Paul Lakeland, *The Liberation of the Laity* (New York: Continuum, 2003) 105.

The pope is elected by the clergy of Rome and all the electors are technically bishops of Rome. The construction is maintained by appointing all cardinals to a parish church in Rome in addition to their official appointment in their own country or elsewhere. This custom only began in the thirteenth century. Prior to that, certainly in the first thousand years of the papacy, the laity of Rome, and especially the civic and political leaders, played an important role in validating the papal election. In the tenth century, dominant Roman families more or less controlled the outcome by means of subterfuge, sexual favours, bribery and force. One of the most notorious was Marozia Theophylacts who appointed and then removed Pope John X, replacing him consecutively with Leo VI and then Stephen VII. She was the mistress of Pope Sergius II whom she also appointed Pope. The sixteenth century historian and disciple of St Philip Neri, Cardinal Baronius called the ninth and tenth century popes, 'invaders of the Holy See, not apostles but apostates'. He went on to say:

> The chief lesson of these times is that the church can get along very well without popes. What is vital to the church's survival is not the pope but Jesus Christ. He is the head of the church, not the pope.[7]

I cite these examples to illustrate that the election process has a history of intrigue and corruption that runs parallel with its undoubted inspiration by the Holy Spirit. There is a well documented history of electors being bought and this simoniacal tradition was declared to be an apostasy by Pope Julius II in 1505, although ironically he himself had been elected in this manner. There have been various attempts at reform leading to the present format of a conclave, which derives from the Latin word for key. (The cardinals were under lock and key, as it were, during the election process. This was an effort to try to protect the electors from outside infuence and to protect the secrecy of the process.) It was Alexander III in 1179 who ruled that the winnining candidate must receive a two thirds majority to be

---

7. See Peter De Rosa, *Vicars of Christ: The Dark Side of the Papacy* (Crown Publishers Inc., 1988) 53 for this quotation from Baronius' *Ecclesiastical Annals.*

elected. He also debarred lay participation by decreeing that only those who were bishop, priest or deacon cardinals could vote. Pope John Paul II changed eight hundred years of precedent by ruling that a simple majority after 33 unsuccessful attempts to secure the two thirds majority would suffice.

Clearly the electoral process has evolved, a product of history, circumstance, machination, divine providence and inspiration. The way it is today is not written in stone. The process is not infallible. It has been open to corruption and manipulation and despite our best wish to think otherwise, it still is. That such a decision is entrusted to a small group of mostly elderly men who have a tenuous and somwhat fabricated link with the clergy of Rome is, to say the least, unusual in our present world. The vesting of such authority in so few could change, perhaps needs to change. That laity have no effective voice in this is an anachronism which belittles the ecclesiology of Vatican II. The notion of collegiality or collaboration or even consultation is not even given lipservice.

This suspicion of the lay voice in effective decision making can be attributed to some of the more sordid historical circumstances where the clergy were effectively dominated or neutered by the ruling lay families. There was a clear need for the church to escape from over invasive control by some of the secular realities. Avery Dulles argues that the resurgence of Roman authority in the nineteenth century was a highpoint in the escape from unwarranted secular control. One of the most significant benefits of this new independence was that it enabled Catholics of different nations to maintain a lively sense of solidarity, even through the two world wars of the twentieth century.[8]

There is considerable merit in Dulles' views. However, the pendulum has perhaps swung too far in the opposite direction. There is too much clerical control, too much clericalism in the way that authority is vested and exercised. It begins in the machinery of a papal election and it is replicated in a host of other procedures which maintain a religious caste in control and prevents, subtley and at times crudely, the emergence of an effective and authoritative lay voice in church governance.

8. Avery Dulles, 'The Papacy for a Globalized Church', *America* vol 183 (July 15th 2000).

Appointment of Bishops

In the church's early centuries no one thought that the Bishop of Rome should name other bishops. Even today no such idea – let alone practice – exists in any of the principal patriarchates of the East. Centralised bishop-naming and its accompanying system of central control is a carry over from an era of political centralism and authoritarianism. There is no pope in the early Christian community and no monarchical bishops operating as local popes in the style they do today.

As church historian Walter Ullmann says, as late as the year 313, 'There was, as yet, no suggestion that the Roman church possessed any legal or constitutional preeminence.' Bishop Leo decided to change that. In a real historical sense, the papacy as we know it is not Petrine, but Leonine. It was Pope Leo I, Bishop in Rome from 440 to 461, a Roman jurist, who cast the Roman episcopate in terms borrowed directly from the Roman imperial court. The one who was called *summus pontifex* (supreme pontiff), who held the *plentitudo potestatis* (the fullness of monarchical power) and the *principatus* (primacy) was the Roman Emperor. Leo grabbed all this language and applied it to himself. As Walter Ullmann says, 'This papal plentitude of power was ... a thoroughly juristic notion, and could be understood only ... against the Roman Law background.'

In today's democratic culture, that recognises the principle of subsidiarity for the whole secular world (including the papacy), this system constitutes a serious case of historical alienation. As Pope John XXIII told us we can, indeed we must, learn from history.[9] A brief survey of some significant developments about the evolution of the church might bring some clarity.

The legal Christian Church

The church that Constantine 'legalised' was the Catholic Church, or Orthodox Christianity. This was actually in 312/313 AD at the Edict of Milan. 325 AD was the first ecumenical council at Nicea. At this time and for another 120 years the universal church was one in faith and no universal bishop had supreme authority. That would not begin to occur until after Leo the

---

9. Pope John XXIII's opening speech, quoted from Abbott, p 712.

Great (450s). In the ancient church the bishops of the apostolic sees of Jerusalem, Antioch and Alexandria were considered to have special authority in the Eastern portion of the church, as Rome did in the West. The Bishop of Rome had authority over his lands only[10] as did all other patriarchs in their own territories. The 'papal structure' was not in place at all and would develop long after Nicaea.

However, Rome has always held a special place in church provenance because it was the see of Peter and this guaranteed it a certain pre-eminence with the churches of the Mediterranean world. Yet, this special dignity was a restrictive rather than an expansive one, even in the West. It afforded the pope certain authoritative licence within peninsular Italy, such as presider at synods, ordainer of bishops, mediator in disputes and discipline enforcer. In other parts of the West, a similar authority was exercised in areas where he had managed to establish vicariates, 'a system of local episcopal representatives through whom they exercised supervision ... These Apostolic Vicars were thought of as sharing the papal care for all the churches and they were given the pallium[11] as a sign of their co-operation in the papal ministry.'[12]

The pope's authority was that of a patriarch of the West (a term which Pope Benedict did not assume on his elevation, as a gesture of reconciliation towards the Eastern Churches) similar

---

10. See canon 6 of Nicaea.
11. 'As the authority of the pope established itself across the churches of the West, it came to be symbolised by the gift of the pallium to the archbishops of the churches of Roman obedience. The pallium is a thin circular stole of white wool embroidered with black crosses. It could and can only be bestowed by the pope. But historically it was more than the pope's livery, it was also a symbol of association with the martyrs of Rome – the wool it was woven from was blessed at the church of St Agnese on her feast-day, and the pallium itself was blessed by being placed overnight on the tomb of St Peter. Power and authority flowed from these holy bones. In all this the pope was secondary. Though the authority of the pope was revered in the West and respected in the East throughout most of the first millennium, nobody came to Rome primarily because the pope was there, but rather for the sake of the holy dead.' Quoted from 'Rome of the Pilgrims', *Faith of Our Fathers* by Eamon Duffy, (Continuum Press 2004) p 93.
12. Ibid., 69.

to the other great sees of Alexandria, Antioch, Jerusalem and Constantinople, each of whom exercised authority over their regions.

Notwitstanding Rome's acknowledged pre-eminence, her engagement with the regional churches was limited. They governed themselves, elected their own bishops, held their own synods, organised their liturgies and the daily life of their churches. Rome, given its historical pedigree, was used as a court of appeal in special circumstances. It was the body of case law built up in such appeals that became the canon law of the church 'and helped shape Western thought about the church, and the central place of the papacy in it.'[13] Those regional churches within the West such as Gaul, Africa, Spain did not experience a hands-on executive authoritative type of governance from Rome. It was more an occasional intervention, usually in response to a local request. Papal authority was mostly used to validate local decisions that were causing some friction.

Elsewhere in the East, Rome had an even more nuanced authority role. As successor to Peter, papal primacy was respected but there were few practical implications for the other patriarchs. Rome was one of the five, the Pentarchy, whose mutual agreement and harmony were the fundamental apostolic underpinning of the church's authority.Within Eastern thought, only if a council was validated by all of the Pentarchy did it acquire the status of a 'general council', whereas in the West papal recognition sufficed. The Roman System came to hold the belief after the Council of Chalcedon (451 AD) that the Roman Patriarch had universal authority in all Christendom. This was violently opposed by all other orthodoxies throughout history. Orientals were slaughtered both by Easterns and Romans for not bowing to this teaching. Ultimately, it would cause a split with the East (1054 AD) when the Patriarch of Constantinople had a dispute with the pope over who had more authority; the Patriarch excommunicated the Pope, who returned the favour, and the 'Orthodox' churches were born.

---

13. Ibid.

Summation of Early Papal Role

In summary of the early papacy, we can say that the pope had three distinct roles or functions. As metropolitan bishop he had a direct immediate involvement in the local churches of Italy; he had a loose patriarchical role as an arbiter or court of appeal for the West; moreover, within the wider church environment he had a Petrine role, a place of honour recognised by all churches of the East and the West, without there being uniform agreement on how this role might be exercised.

Eamon Duffy, Professor of the History of Christianity in the University of Cambridge, is an eminent church historian, who has done extensive research into the evolution of the papacy. In his view 'much of the history of the papacy has been the collapsing of these three distinct roles into each other, and the growing claims of the popes to exercise all three functions as if they all involved metropolitan authority everywhere – as if the promises to Peter made the popes, in effect, archbishops of every province.'[14]

Much of what we consider most characteristic of the modern Petrine office has accrued to the pope through the merging of previously distinct functions and the accidents of history. The present papal authority in the appointment of the episcopate was not always a given. It changed in the past and could also change in the future.The papacy in its present form is the work of history and circumstance as much as it is of divine intention.

There are significant issues surfacing about how papal authority is wielded in the church and one of the most significant debates over the past decades has been whether the local church existed before the universal church or *vice versa*, and what is the relationship of the local to the universal. This is not just a theoretical question because it has huge implications for how authority is exercised within the church. It has a fundamental bearing on how the church is governed.

---

14. Ibid., 70.

CHAPTER 5

Universal Pre-eminence

Prior to his elevation to the papacy, the then Cardinal Ratzinger found himself engaged in a robust series of debates with another leading theologian, Cardinal Kasper on this very issue. Cardinal Ratzinger, in a paper that he presented at the World Congress of Ecclesial Communities in 1998, outlined an historical overview from which he deduced his conclusions. In his analysis, the early apostles proclaimed the message of Christ without any geographical restrictions; their mission field was the whole world, 'to the ends of the earth' (Acts 1:8) and to make disciples of all men (cf Mt 28:19). The apostles were not bishops of particular local churches, but assigned to the whole world and to the whole church; the universal church thus preceded the local churches, which arose as its concrete realisations.[1] He argues that Paul did not see himself as a bishop of a particular place, and the initial division of labour of Paul and Barnabas for the Gentiles and James, Peter and Cephas for the Jews was soon superseded.

Organisation and Structure

These new churches required leadership at local level and, of necessity, organisation and structure naturally arose within the local situations. Thus two forms, the universal mission and the local apostolate, co-existed side by side in the nascent church. This structure continued well into the second century when the demands of the local churches saw the emergence of a tripartite division of bishop, priest and deacon. Irenaeus of Lyons testifies that the bishops now understood that they were the successors of the apostles.[2]

---

1. See Joseph Ratzinger, *Called to Communion. Understanding the Church Today*, (San Francisco: Ignatius Press, 1996) 75-104.
2. Irenaeus, *Adv. Haer*. V, 11:1.

However, with the development of the episcopal ministry, the ministries of the universal church gradually disappeared in the course of the second century. According to Ratzinger, 'This was a development not only historically inevitable but theologically necessary; it brought to light the unity of the sacrament and the intrinsic unity of the apostolic service.'[3]

As head of the Congregation for the Doctrine of the Faith, Cardinal Ratzinger's position was that the universal church came first, and as the papacy is of the essence of the universal church, then the papacy came first too. Moreover, Ratzinger contends that the contest in the West over the freedom of the church from the state under Gregory VII (d. 1057) and the conflict with the mendicant orders in the thirteenth century highlighted the Petrine role as guarantor of spiritual resurgence. Only the universal church can ensure the separation of the particular church from the state and society. Today too, we are experiencing the phenomenon of apostolic movements coming 'from below' and transcending the local church: movements in which new charisms are emerging and animating the local pastoral ministry. Today too, such movements, which cannot be derived from the episcopal principle, find their theological and practical justification in primacy.[4]

How one interprets this issue of the local and the universal is more than just a question of historical sequence. It affects the way the church's fundamental design is understood. If one accepts Ratzinger's rationale, it places the papacy in charge of the church. Because they came after the universal church, the local churches, each led by its own bishop, are subordinate to the papacy. For all sorts of things they might want to do – indeed, believe in all conscience they ought to do – they need Rome's permission first. It is often not forthcoming. In brief, according to Ratzinger, one can say that early church history bears unequivocal testimony that the apostolic ministry was a universal one which in turn gave rise to the establishment of local churches. It is all the more dramatic, therefore, that a serious challenge to this theory of church structure has been mounted not from some

3. Ratzinger, 'The Ecclesial Movements; a Theological Reflection on Their Place in the Church', 37.
4. *Forum Katholischer Theologie* 2 (1986): 81-96.

progressive academic campus but by the head of the Pontifical Council for Christian Unity, Cardinal Kasper, who has challenged the basic Ratzinger proposition that the universal church came first.[5]

Local takes precedence

On 23 April 2001, *America* magazine drew attention to an unusual public disagreement within the Vatican by printing on its cover two photographs of prominent cardinals, Ratzinger and Kasper. One installment of Cardinal Kasper's argument with Cardinal Ratzinger had originally appeared in a German theological magazine.[6] But when an English interpretation appeared in *America*, provided by Professor Ladislas Orsy SJ of Georgetown University Law Centre, Washington DC, some of the remarks attributed to Cardinal Kasper were publicly challenged by Cardinal Avery Dulles as having been embroidered in translation. So *The Tablet*, because of the importance of knowing exactly what Cardinal Kasper was saying, commissioned its own more literal translation from Robert Nowell.[8]

Professor Orsy later joined the debate himself, arguing that the Vatican curia's behaviour since the end of the Second Vatican Council in 1965 has largely nullified what was intended to be the Council's most important doctrinal achievement, its doctrine of collegiality. This nicely dovetails with the Kasper analysis. Both of them point to the urgent need to reinforce the weight given to the local churches, in the internal affairs of each of them and in the government of the church regionally and as a whole. And this is not just for the sake of good will but because it is necessary in order to respect the inalienable rights and responsibilities of local bishops. They are not delegates of Rome. They are empowered directly by their sacramental orders. Collegiality comes from Christ, not from the dispensations of the curia. And a church without papacy *and* collegiality is unbalanced.

---

5. Robert Leicht, 'Cardinals in conflict', *The Tablet* (April 28, 2001) 607-608.

6. The German text of this article was originally published in the journal *Stimmen der Zeit* (December 2000).

7. The translation appeared in *America* (23 April 2001) 16-17.

8. This translation appeared in *The Tablet* (23 June 2001) 927-930.

In 1999 Kasper, in his historical review of the first millennium, concluded that the ecclesiology of this period 'excluded a one-sided emphasis on the local churches as well as a one-sided emphasis on the universal church.'[9] In his judgement, the priority of the universal over the local has been a characteristic of the Latin Church since the onset of the second millennium, ever since the Latin Patriachate (based in Rome) lost the counter-weight of the Greek patriarchs (based in Constantinople and elsewhere) after the Great Schism of 1054. The West alone developed a new conception of church that put the emphasis on universality. This caused a trend to develop which attributed all authority to the pope. Undoubtedly this doctrine was crucial in the fight against conciliarism, the Protestant Reformation, state absolutism, Gallicanism and Josephism. The First Vatican Council with its teaching on the primacy of jurisdiction of the pope, reinforced it, as did the 1917 *Code of Canon Law*.

The Second Vatican Council sought to recover the beliefs and attitudes of the early church and to harmonise them with the teachings of the First Vatican Council. The council quite properly called for inculturation, collegiality and a renewed emphasis on the local church as a centre of pastoral life and worship. The enactments regarding the sacramental character of episcopal ordination and episcopal collegiality bear testimony to this. Subsequently the Extraordinary Synod of Bishops stated that communion was the central and foundational idea of the Second Vatican Council. Later in 1992 the Congregation for the Doctrine of Faith, in a letter to the bishops, objected to a one-sided ecclesiology which attributed excessive weight to the local churches to the detriment of the universal. However, in Kasper's view, they went beyond the teaching of the Vatican II by asserting that the local churches exist 'in and from' the universal church and they proposed the ontological and historical priority of the universal church. Congar also believed that Vatican II ecclesiology recognised anew the reality and the significance of the local church.

This represents a movement away from an ecclesiology concerned simply with the universal church and the expansion of one church – the Church of Rome – throughout the world and

9. Walter Kasper, 'On the Church: A Friendly Reply to Cardinal Ratzinger', *The Furrow*, (June 2001) 323-332.

forgetful of the reality of the local churches; in other words, an ecclesiology oriented towards a uniform universality which is pragmatically divided into dioceses. Yves Congar believed that this was the most fundamentally new and promising contribution made by the Council.[10] In essence, Kasper took issue with the Congregation for the Doctrine of the Faith's position that 'the universal church is a reality ontologically and temporally prior to every individual particular church.'[11] Kasper felt that Rome too quickly responds to local problems by direct intervention, but not always with pastoral sensitivity. Many people 'can no longer understand universal church regulations and simply ignore them.'[12] He calls it a 'mental and practical schism'.[13] He stresses that he is not challenging legal or doctrinal structures but a particular style of leadership and a theological interpretation. When the exercise of primacy is largely centred on Roman decisions and decrees, is it not then the case that 'the authority and the initiative of the college (of bishops) is practically reduced to a naked fiction'?[14]

The 'Letter on Certain Aspects of the Church Understood as Communion'[15] makes clear that in the situation among the Eastern Orthodox Communities, although their local churches may be considered as true particular churches, nonetheless their existence as such churches is wounded because of their deprivation of full communion with the universal church represented and realised through the Petrine officeholder.[16] The First Vatican Council stigmatised as heretical a unilateral concentration on either the total episcopate or the papacy. The pope can in his

10. Yves Congar, *Le Concile de Vatican II*, (Paris: Beauchesne 1984) 24.
11. Congregation for the Doctrine of the Faith, 'Letter on Certain Aspects of the Faith Understood as Communion,' *Origins* 22 (25 June 1992) 108-12 # 8.
12. Walter Kasper, 'The Universal Church and the Local Church: A Friendly Rejoinder,' in idem, *Leadership in the Chuch: How Traditional Roles Can Serve the Christian Community Today*, trs Brian McNeil (New York: Crossroads/Herder and Herder, 2003) 158.
13. Ibid.
14. Kasper, '*Theologie und Praxis*,' 42, quoted in McDonnell, 'Ratzinger/Kasper' 230.
15. Ibid.
16. Nichols 221.

own right speak infallibly, and does not need to appeal to a council but the bishops are not just papal administrators; the episcopate is also of divine right that no pope can set aside. Church and pope cannot be set over against each other but need to exist in a relational unity in order to complement each other. The pope as guardian of the faith and practice does not displace the local bishop but 'confirms, supplements and sometimes corrects their efforts'.[17] At the same time, the local bishop, whose particular church is itself the church in miniature, brings the experience of an often far-flung community to the Petrine, from where their concerns can be mediated to the rest of the church universal. The local and the universal church interpenetrate in an unbreakable exchange, a kind of *perichoresis*, similar to that of the persons in the Trinity. Within the western tradition this is graphically captured in the Eucharist, which is celebrated *una cum* (one with) the pope as well as the local bishop.

Though the papacy is not a sacramental order, it can be called a charismatic order;[18] it is not separate from the regular ministry which all bishops share but it is unique in its mode of continuity and in the personal authority conferred by the charism of the papal office. Ultimately, this *perichorsis* is a mystery and requires a journey of faith into the mystery of unity, notwithstanding the tensions that are evident.

What this debate shows is that authority and governance is not a static reality. Tensions exist because authority is a living dynamic reality that is validated by life or rejected by it. Advocates of the universal position are probably more comfortable in the pre-Vatican II model, while the local supporters seek greater autonomy to create a more vibrant, freer local expression of church. Authority has evolved, as has the exercise of governance. If one considers the secular world, authority in the past was often affected by the threat of physical punishment which was once normative in schools and homes. Today, that form of authority would be seen as abusive and repulsive. Likewise, the church in the past spoke in terms of anathemas or dire consequences for those who dissented; today such warnings are archaic and counter productive.

17. Ibid., 232.
18. Ibid., 233.

Balance

Nichols, while mostly supportive of the universal position, also seeks to bring balance to the debate. This is difficult to achieve because this very issue raises the relationship of authority and the precise nature of the Petrine ministry within the *collegium* of bishops. There is always the danger that a particularist view of the church, which exalts the rights of the local church, would damage the universality of the church.

> In particularist ecclesiology the whole church is present in a particular church; in universalist ecclesiology, by contrast, the whole church is present only in the integration of all the particular churches. If one thinks the universal church from a particularist ecclesiology, one has the idea of the communion of churches; through participation in this communion, the particular churches express or 'focus' the being of the entire church. If, however, one thinks the particular churches from a universalist ecclesiology, one understands the local church as a portion of the People of God, existing through incorporation into the church universal.[19]

There has been a strong tendency under the pontificate of Pope John Paul II to promote 'a theory of the universal church that exalts its central structures and authority (of their nature basically clerical) *over against* local communities and *their* inherent authority (of their nature fundamentally lay).'[20] In the universalist view no local community came into existence by its own efforts. It was a gift from God 'in an historical setting prepared by a variety of social structures and relationships.'[21] In this mindset, faith often is seen as a package that is handed on from God to the apostles and on through their successors. They seem to miss out on the immeasurable number of ordinary Christians who hand on the faith in their local communities.

There is a natural tension that is unavoidable but not necessarily destructive. Some commentators have seen it as a 'dual-

---

19. Aidan Nichols, Epiphany, *A Theological Introduction to Catholicism*, (Collegeville, Minnesota: Liturgical Press, 1996) 220.
20. William A. Clark, *A Voice of Their Own, The Authority of the Local Parish*, (Collegeville, Minnesota: Liturgical Press, 2005) 190.
21. Ibid.

ism'[22] which gives the impression of two incompatible principles struggling for supremacy. Yet, because it is the one and the
same Spirit who dwells in the members and enlivens the local
community and also raises up central structures and offices,
these different *loci* of authority are inseparably united. It is the
same Spirit who generates the wine of enthusiasm and impetus
and the sobriety of caution and prudence.

---

22. Paul M. Grammont and Philibert Zobel, 'The Authority of the
Indwelling word,' in John M. Todd, ed., *Problems of Authority*
(Baltimore: Helicon; London: DLT, 1962) 87.

CHAPTER 6

Magisterium

Central to the any examination of authority within the Catholic Church is the role of the magisterium. It too has evolved over time and it has acquired nuances and interpretations that have been added in response to circumstances. Its functioning is many faceted and delicate, and the range and scope of its remit and the power devolved to members within its hierarchical structure is, to say the least, problematic.

What is it?
The word magisterium means the authority of the master or teacher.[1] It was rarely used in the early church and in the Middle Ages it was applied equally to the office and authority of teachers, both bishops and scholars. Thomas Aquinas spoke of the *magisterium cathedrae pastoralis* (the authority of the bishop and the pastoral chair) and the *magisterium cathedrae magistralis* (the authority of the theologian and the teaching chair). By the nineteenth century it had narrowed to be used almost exclusively as a reference to the teaching authority of the bishop, commonly expressed by the episcopal college under the headship of the pope.[2]

The Catholic model posits the existence of a divinely created institution, the Roman Catholic Church, which is 'in' the world but not fully 'of' it, which serves as the nexus between the other-world and the this-world, which stands both above man and

---

1. See Yves Congar, 'A Semantic History of the Term 'Magisterium'' and 'A Brief History of the Forms of the Magisterium and its Relations with Scholars,' in *Readings in Moral Theology No 3: The Magisterium and Morality*, Charles E. Curran and Richard A. McCormick, eds., (New York: Paulist, 1982), 297 -313 and 314- 331.
2. See Richard Gaillardetz, *By What Authority* (Collegeville, Minnesota: Liturgical Press, 2003) 60.

permeates man through the sacraments and which directs his earthly activity, and without whose assistance individual salvation of an eternal, otherworldly nature is hard to attain.

Within this mindset, the doctrine of the apostolic succession attributes to the hierarchy, and those commissioned or approved by them, a genuine teaching authority, technically called 'magisterium'. Catholics believe that the supreme power in the church resides in the whole episcopate, the college of bishops with and under the Bishop of Rome, who is the spokesperson for the college as well as the focal point of unity for the whole church.[3]

According to the Catechism, the magisterium is the teaching body of the church, which is charged with 'the solemn command of Christ from the apostles to announce the saving truth' (CCC 2032). It is made up of the pope and those bishops in communion with him, who are 'authentic teachers' of the faith, making up the ordinary magisterium by their preaching and catechesis (CCC 2034). These bishops are assisted by their brother priests as well as by lay faithful, 'theologians and spiritual authors' who assist with catechesis and formation (CCC 2033).

We are reminded that the magisterium 'is not superior to the Word of God (scripture and tradition), but is its servant. All that it proposes ... is drawn from this single deposit of faith' (CCC 86). It can be said, therefore, that the life of the church extends not from the magisterium, but rather that the magisterium extends from the life of the church. The faithful 'have the right to be instructed' in the matters of the magisterium by their bishops through their pastors. The faithful, then, in addition to this right, 'have the *duty* of observing the constitutions and decrees conveyed by the legitimate authority of the church' (CCC 2037).

To and Fro
When the bishops define the faith, as they can do by their corporate action, they are trustworthy witnesses. The Vatican document refers to 'the sure charism of truth'. The teachings of the magisterium represent the fullest expression of the truth of

---

3. James J. Bacik, *Catholic Spirituality, Its History and Challenge* (Mahwah, NJ: Paulist Press, 2002) 128.

Roman Catholicism. One of the great theologians of the last century, Hans urs Von Balthasar speaks of the church hierarchy as 'crystallised love.'[4]

However, when the magisterium becomes distant or removed from the daily fabric of church life it becomes endangered. It can end up conducting a monologue within a clerical and, at times, a rarefied mindset that has lost contact with the authentic voice of the faithful. The dialogical nature of the magisterium's search for truth is extremely delicate and within church literature one can see clearly an uncertain wavering between two positions.

On the one hand, there is an acceptance that the relationship between the faithful and the magisterium is a complex and important one. The deposit of faith is entrusted to the whole church and is handed on in the 'teaching, life, and worship' of the whole church (*DV* 8/10). Thus it is from the life of the faithful, and from their faith-consciousness (*sensus fidelium*) that the magisterium must draw the teachings it proposes as revealed truth. The faithful are not simply to passively follow each teaching. If the magisterium presents what seems to be a new teaching, it is the role of the Holy Spirit to aid the faithful in recognising the truth of the teaching. So, reception of a teaching matters. The faithful share actively in the role of the magisterium, because it is the whole People of God that 'clings without fail to the faith once delivered to the saints, penetrates it more deeply by accurate insights, and applies it more thoroughly to life' (*LG* 12).

On the other hand, the magisterium has the responsibility to preserve the unity of the church and the faith and at times must be able to demand obedience: 'However much the sacred magisterium avails itself of the contemplation, life, and study of the faithful, its office is not reduced merely to ratifying the assent already expressed by the latter; indeed in the interpretation and explanation of the written or transmitted Word of God, the magisterium can anticipate or demand their assent.' (CDF, *Mysterium Ecclesiae*, 1973).

Such polarities of interpretation can easily lend themselves to tension and/or confusion. Holding them in respectful dialogue,

---

4. Hans Urs von Balthasar, *Church and World* (New York: Herder and Herder, 1967) 27.

without letting any one dominate, has proven to be problematic. Being magisterial is not easy! The bishops are not simply mouthpieces for the pope nor are they mouthpieces for the opinions of their flock as evidenced in the latest polls. Each bishop has been given the sure charism of truth and uniquely he is called to exercise that charism faithfully. He is both a *testis fidei*, a witness to the faith which is professed by those in his community, and the authoritative teacher and judge of the faith, responsible to safeguard it against distortion or error.

Yet, Christianity recognises only one absolute authority – that of God himself. This means that all the secondary authorities are subject to criticism and correction. Every created channel that manifests God and brings men to him is capable also of misleading men and turning them away from God. Michael Paul Gallagher speaks of the young church today being a people of experience as opposed to an older church which he characterises as a church of experience. Today all authority, religious and secular, is put under the microscope in the light of experience. Unless the experience of authority is coherent it will be simply rejected.

In the pre-Vatican II church, authority was largely central, uniform, rigid and hierarchical. Post-Vatican II there was a huge resistance to such a structure. As early as 1968 Cardinal Heenan wrote in *The Tablet* of May 18:

> Today what the pope says is by no means accepted as authoritative by all Catholic theologians ... The decline of the magisterium is one of the most significant developments in the post-conciliar church.

American theologian Richard McCormick echoed this view:

> I believe it is safe to say that the hierarchical magisterium is in deep trouble. For many of the educated faithful it has ceased to be truly credible.[5]

Even Pope John Paul II himself recognised this reality in *Pastores Dabo Vobis*:

> There are also worrying and negative factors within the church herself which have a direct influence on the lives and

---

5. *Proceedings of the Catholic Theological Society of America*, vol 24 (1970) 251.

ministry of priests. For example: the lack of due knowledge of the faith among many believers; a catechesis which has little practical effect ..., an incorrectly understood pluralism in theology, culture and pastoral teaching which ... ends up by hindering ecumenical dialogue and threatening the necessary unity of faith; a persisitent diffidence towards and almost unacceptance of the magisterium of the hierarchy; the one-sided tendencies which reduce the riches of the gospel's message and transform the proclamation and witness to the faith into an element of exclusively human and social liberation or into an alienating flight into superstition and religiosity without (§7).'[6]

Relevance of Magisterium to Life

One of the big issues facing the magisterium is its relevance to the lives of its members. Tensions exist today between those who affirm the legitimacy of both the Catholic conception of the magisterium and of what Avery Dulles in his *Models of the Church* has termed the 'institutional model' of the Catholic Church, and others who present a 'People of God' model which posits a unilinear evolutionary understanding of the future of the Catholic Church with the ultimate supremacy of individual conscience.

A pre-Vatican II theology would have stressed that orthodoxy requires the subordination of the insights of philosophy (whether classical or modern) or the social sciences and humanities to 'official' Catholic theology. For example, St Thomas Aquinas's theology is considered orthodox because he co-opted Aristotle's views into the Catholic view and not the other way around. Put simply, St Thomas incorporated Greek reason within a Christian faith, Greek cyclical thought within Christian revelation, Greek human nature within Christian grace, Greek fate within Christian responsibility and freedom and the Greek emphasis on the eternal within the Christian emphasis on the divine.

---

6. John Paul II, *Pastores Dabo Vobis: On the Formation of Priests in the Circumstances of the Present Day*, March 25, 1992; *L'Observatore Romano*, English, April 8, 1992.

Pope John XXIII suggested a new departure when he spoke of the church as being a part of history and needing to recognise that she could learn from history. He castigated those people who 'behave as though history, which teaches us about life, had nothing to teach them'. He said that we must recognise the mysterious designs of Divine Providence working through people and events – even those events which seem, to conflict with the aims of the church.The church could no longer engage in a monologue but had to initiate a respectful dialogue with the world. The church was not to to be outside history or uncritically resist change. It must always be listening to what the Spirit is saying in the hearts of people and in the events of history.[7]

Broadly speaking, one could say that previously the official teaching concentrated on the institutional church whereas more recent approaches focus on the church as a movement, as something that must grow in history, as basically eschatological in purpose. In simple terms, we had been accustomed to viewing the church mainly as an instituition with an eschatological halo around its juridical structures, whilst now we see it as a Christ-founded and Spirit-borne movement which the institution must serve, not dominate. This corresponds to what was said about the magisterium in the interpretation of scripture in *Dei Verbum* – 'it was not superior to the word of God but ministers to the same word by teaching only what has been handed on to it' (*DV* 10). The Council reminds us that through baptism and confirmation all Christians are qualified and commissioned to testify to the truth. They are not merely recipients of faith but are actively involved in the witness to faith.

Avery Dulles' Perspective

One of the major theologians who spans the pre- and post-Vatican II era is Avery Dulles. He has written extensively on this issue of authority in many of his books and articles, yet he too seems unable to come to a clear decision. He vacillates between the older acceptance of magisterium and a much more radical interpretation. At one level, he argues not only for a pluralis-ation of authentic authorities within the Catholic Church – which in and by itself is acceptable – but refuses to grant the

7. Pope John XXIII's opening speech, quoted from Abbott, 712.

magisterium any special or privileged status among the various other authorities. He states boldly: 'The official magisterium is only one of the many elements in the total witness of the church.'[8] He points out that 'there are limits to hierarchical authority.'[9] In this regard, Dulles accepts Cardinal John Henry Newman's argument in his *Via Media* (1877) that the church inherits from Christ three distinct offices, the priestly, the prophetic, and the royal. For Dulles, 'the overall performance of the church results from a continual interaction of the three offices, whose bearers, having different abilities and concerns, cooperate and occasionally check one another's excesses … The royal power of the pastors, Newman concluded, must function in tension with the unofficial authority of saints and scholars, who in turn stand in some tension with one another.'[10] The role of the theologian, then, is 'at the service of 'this believing effort to understand the faith'' (*Veritatis Splendor* 109). 'He does this in communion with the magisterium' (*Donum Veritatis* 82).

How these diverse elements function together and which of them, if any, has definitive authority is the core issue. Dulles argues for the absolute necessity of input from the non-magisterial elements of the church but sees the hierarchy's role as one which is called to 'recognise, encourage, coordinate, and judge the gifts and initiatives of others.' The complete text is as follows:

> The church is greatly blessed by her sacramental structures, which mediate to her members the fullness of God's gift in Christ. But these structures must be rightly used. They are intended to help the faithful develop their personal powers and gifts, whether of prayer, of understanding, or of action. If all initiative is left to the highest office-holders – the bishops – not even they can function well. Their proper role is not to initiate all action, but rather to recognise, encourage, coordinate, and judge the gifts and initiatives of others. Where the community is inert, the hierarchy becomes paralysed.

---

8. Avery Dulles, *The Survival of Dogma* (New York: Crossroad, 1971) 100.
9. Avery Dulles SJ, *The Catholicity of the Church* (London: The Clarendon Press, 1985) 121.
10. Ibid., 122.

Having no material on which to work, it is forced to be idle or to assume functions not properly its own.[11]

Different Kinds of Authority

Dulles contends that in most Christian bodies, several types of authority exist concurrently. On the one hand, there is the juridical and public authority of the highest officers – whether pope, bishops, or ruling bodies, such as assemblies, synods, and councils. These officials make their authority felt, normally by issuing documents, which are regarded as normative for the group. On the other hand, there are private authorities, which in their own way are no less important than the officials. Under this heading one would have to include, first, scholars, who speak on the basis of their research and professional competence. Secondly, there are 'charismatic persons' who seem to be endowed with a more than common measure of the true Christian spirit. Like the prophets of old, these charismatics often feel impelled to criticise the officials and scholars, to rebuke them for their infidelity and insensitivity. Finally, there is the authority of consensus. In the church, public opinion is definitely a force to be reckoned with, especially in the democratic age.[12]

The benefit of 'this plurality of authentic Christian sources,' for Dulles, is that it

protects the believer from being crushed by the weight of any single authority; it restrains any one organ from so imposing itself as to eliminate what the others have to say. It provides a margin of liberty within which each individual can feel encouraged to make his own distinctive contribution, to understand the faith in a way proper to himself. And at the same time it provides the church as a whole with the suppleness it needs to operate in different parts of the globe and in a rapidly changing world.[13]

However, Dulles affirms that notwithstanding all the merits of pluralism we must also acknowledge that it too has its limits and dangers. If the word of God cannot be totally identified with

---

11. Ibid., 125-126.
12. Ibid., 84.
13. Ibid., 88.

any particular expression, it by no means follows that every human attitude and expression is consonant with the gospel of Christ ... Thus it remains an important task of ecclesiastical authority to see to it that ... the ongoing transformations of Christian life do not undermine the apostolicity and catholic unity essential to the church.[14]

Surprisingly and somewhat confusingly, Dulles can also simply state that 'only the bearers of the official magisterium can formulate judgements in the authoritative way. They may, of course, accept and approve the work of private theologians, but when they do so it is they – not the theologians who give official status to the theories they approve.'[15]

In *The Resilient Church* (1977) Dulles argues against those conservatives who, through fear or complacency, baulk at adapting the doctrines and institutions of the church to the times in which we live; equally, he opposes those liberals whose programmes of adaptation are based on an uncritical acceptance of the norms and slogans of western secularist ideologies.[16] Dulles sought for both/and rather than either/or. He saw the potential in fusing the daring of the liberal with the caution of the conservative, the openness of the liberal with the fidelity of the conservative.

The pastoral office, charismatically exercised, fosters other charisms in the church while correcting their deviations. The special charism of the pastoral office is not to replace or diminish other charisms but to bring them to their fullest efficacy. This involved several distinct functions.

1. First, the pastoral office must authenticate genuine charisms and distinguish them from false charisms.
2. Second, hierarchical leaders have the function of stimulating and encouraging the charisms.
3. Third, the pastors must direct the charisms according to the norm of apostolic faith and thus bring them into subjection to the law of the cross.
4. Finally, office, as a kind of general charisma, has the responsibility of coordinating all the particular charisms so that

14. Ibid., 90-91.
15. Ibid., 100-101.
16. Avery Dulles, *The Resilient Church: The Necessity and Limits of Adaptation* (New York: Doubleday, 1977) 5-6.

they may better achieve the goal of building up the total body of Christ.

The pastoral office prevents the prior unity of the church from being fragmented by the free responses of the enthusiasts, and reminds the spiritually gifted of their duty to obey the one Lord of the church. The characteristic temptation of the free charismatic is to follow the momentary impulses arising out of the transitory local situation, without sufficient regard for the established order and for universal, long-term need. The pastoral office therefore integrates the possibly distorted self-sufficiency of the particular charisms into the greater unity of ecclesial love.[17]

Dulles reasserts the special guardian function of the magisterium in *A Church to Believe In: Discipleship and the Dynamics of Freedom* (1983). In the second chapter, 'Institution and Charism in the Church,' Dulles denies that 'charisma' and 'institution' or 'spirit' and 'structure' stand in a zero-sum relationship to each other:

> It is often said that the last word lies with the office-holders, since it is their function to discern between true and false charisms – a point made more than once in the Constitution of the Church. The presumption does lie with the hierarchy, but the presumption cannot be absolutised ... Thus there is no ultimate juridical solution to collisions between spiritually gifted reformers and conscientious defenders of the accepted order. The church is not a totalitarian system in which disagreement can be ended by simple fiat.[18]

Finally, mention should be made of an essay of Avery Dulles entitled 'Community of Disciples as a Model of the Church' which was published in 1986.[19] In this essay, Dulles, building on Chapter One of his previously referred to *A Church to Believe In* (1983), offers yet a sixth model of the church, i.e. the 'community of disciples' that, in Richard McBrien's words, 'retrieves and synthesises the positive features of the other five models with-

17. Dulles, *A Church to Believe In*, op. cit., 1983, 35-36.
18. Ibid., 37-38.
19. Avery Dulles,'Community of Disciples as a Model of Church,' in *Philosophy and Theology*, vol 1, no 2, (Winter, 1986) 99-120.

out carrying forward their respective liabilities.'[20] Pastoral leadership, as we know from the New Testament and from Christian tradition, involves something more than the formal authority of office – i.e. the mere fact of being duly installed. Those selected for pastoral office are previously judged to have both the vocation and the aptitude, and if they are ordained they receive in addition the grace of the sacrament. They therefore possess not only the juridical authority of office but personal and charismatic authority.

The Modern Dilemma

That a scholar such as Dulles has difficulty pinning down a precise understanding of the role of the magisterium merely underlines the problems facing the church. At one level we can see that any blind acceptance of church rulings is gone forever, no matter how well informed or how perfectly articulated. We live in questioning times where modern people doubt both the medium and the message. The individual has become his/her own arbiter of truth. He/she trusts his/her own instincts and is suspicious of the external voice of authority. The 'have it' and 'do it my way' mentality rules. For many it has become the mantra of our age, the age of the unencumbered ego where an expensive hair do is justified in glossy ads because 'I'm worth it', or I can indulge in a Big Mac Meal any way I want because 'I'm loving it'.

Yet this is not the full picture and at another level we see the individual frightened by the mayhem of life, less than satisfied by the ephemeral pleasures of the hedonistic culture all round us. We see him/her not as the arbiter of truth but ultimately questioned by Truth itself. In such a predicament he/she looks for certitude and is attracted to fundamentalism as a solution to the angst that is gripping him/her. Answers of a definitive kind bring solace and the magisterium can be the antidote to the incoherence of life. In the words of T. S. Eliot, 'This is the greatest treason , To do the right deed for the wrong Reason' (*Murder in The Cathedral*).

---

20. Richard P. McBrien, *Caesar's Coin: Religion and Politics in America* (New York: Macmillan, 1987) 46.

Others rail against an authority that they believe to be auto-cratic and unbending and the preserve of an unelected clerical caste. They posit the scaredness of conscience and cite Thomas Aquinas who defended the ultimate authority of the informed conscience.

However, Ratzinger is suspicious of those who too easily use the conscience argument as a kind of 'get out' clause. He has long been a critic of those who seek to conform Catholicism to the relativist mindset. He warns that 'No longer is conscience understood as that knowledge which derives from a higher form of knowing. It is instead the individual's self determin-ation which may not be directed by someone else, a determin-ation by which each person decides for himself what is moral in a given situation.'[21]

This relativist self actualising notion of religious freedom as-sumes an understanding of conscience that separates itself from any norms in grace or nature. As a consequence of this flawed thinking, one is left with a separation that leaves conscience not as the judge of what is moral on the basis of the order of things but as itself the creator of what is right. Conscience has moved from its rightful place as ultimate judge to its wrongful place as creator or author of rules and norms. Ratzinger would agree with the Catholic theologian William E. May in his essay on the 'Catholic Principles of Scholarship and Learning' when he states the more traditional view of the authority of the magisterium:

> Because the magisterium always teaches with an authority that the Catholic respects as more than human in origin, the committed Catholic will have a connatural eagerness to ac-cept all that the magisterium teaches ... This connatural eagerness and a willingness to give a 'religious assent of soul' do not, however, at least in my opinion, exclude the possibility of raising questions and suggesting hypotheses that may be in contradiction to magisterial teachings, provided that in raising questions and suggesting alternatives the Catholic scholar 1) can appeal to other magisterial teachings

---

21. Josef Ratzinger, 'Address to European Doctrinal Commission,' at Luxembourg (Vienna), May 1989, *Christian Order* 31 (February 1990) 108.

more certainly and definitively taught with which the scholar thinks the teachings questioned are incompatible, and 2) is willing to submit his conclusions to the judgement of the magisterium. Moreover, in proposing hypotheses and alternatives, the Catholic scholar must not claim that fellow Catholics are free to set aside magisterial teachings and put his own opinions in their place. One's own opinions are surely not infallible, and Catholics ought never to prefer the opinions of scholars, however learned, to the authoritative teachings of those to whom our Lord has given the right and responsibility to speak in his name.[22]

By the light of Christ inherent in each person, the conscience is used to determine naturally and rationally many of the moral truths of the church. However, 'personal conscience and reason should not be set in opposition to the moral law or the magisterium of the church' (CCC 2039). J.H. Newman said that one could describe the church's teaching role as making explicit what is already implicit within each conscience.

Ecumenical Dimension
Richard John Neuhaus , in his deceptively titled *The Catholic Moment*, states that for many Catholics today, the efforts of Pope John Paul II, Joseph Ratzinger (now Pope Benedict XVI) and the Extraordinary Synod were an attempt to turn back; to others an effort to rescue the institutional remains of an authority that is no longer plausible; to yet others an effort to chart a course of faithfulness in the absence of false certitudes that once put their leadership beyond question. In Neuhaus' view, which he considers an ecumenical perspective, 'one must hope that the last is the accurate reading of what they intend'.[23]

---

22. William E. May, 'Catholic Principles of Scholarship and Learning,' *Homiletic and Pastoral Review*, (February, 1988) 14-15.
23. Richard John Neuhaus, *The Catholic Moment: The Paradox of the Church in the Postmodern World* (New York: Harper and Row, 1987) 125.

CHAPTER 7

Sensus Fidelium

In recent decades a persistent clamour has prevailed about the institutional church's disregard for a key aspect of discernment within the church, namely the *sensus fidelium* (sense of the faithful). This refers to a core element of our faith, namely that there exists within the whole body of the church a sense of the faithful around the truth of the content of the faith. Inherent is an acceptance that the whole body of Christ has a role to play in discerning the truth. All the baptised have received the Holy Spirit and all are enlightened with the spirit of truth. When the whole body coalesces in unity around an aspect of faith, this is a clear and authoritative sign.

In seeking to rediscover this sense of the faithful tradition that historically was so critical a part of the church's discernment about faith issues, the teaching in the Dogmatic Constitution on the Church, art 12, recalled that 'supernatural sense of the faith' that equips all in the church for the task of proclaiming the gospel. Though the teaching clearly represented a rediscovery of the role and importance of the *sensus fidelium* by the bishops of Vatican II, it was not their intent that it be used to create a separate body of teachers among the laity, agitating for such changes in the church as democratisation, the ordination of women, change on the church's position regarding artificial birth control, etc.

Yet if one examines article 10 of the Dogmatic Constitution on Divine Revelation and then looks at art 12 and 35, one can see the wisdom of the Council fathers' approach. It situates all of the church, hierarchy and laity, in a listening role, attending to the Word of God. Only after hearing the word are any distinctions made between roles and responsibilities. Because the responsibility to listen, to receive, to grow in understanding, and transmit the Word of God pertains to all in the church, all need to participate in this process. In particular, this means that the hierarchy is not free to ignore the *sensus fidelium*, which represents a true 'theological resource' (*locus theologicus*), and that concretely it must create the appropriate institutional means for the laity to express themselves.

Unfortunately, this has remained largely a theoretical construct and rarely has it been a priority within the mindset of the hierarchy. The absence of official, informed dialogue has led to the arrival of movements in America such as the 'Petition of the People of the Church' and 'Voice of the Faithful'. In Europe a major lay reform group was established under the umbrella title 'We are the Church' in Austria in 1996 and a movement called 'Australian Reforming Catholics' was established in 2001. In many instances, exaggerated forms of democratic action in the church have been expressions of a sense of frustration by the laity at not being listened to by the hierarchy, who bear a significant responsibility for this situation by their failure to foster real dialogue in the church. There needs to be much more attention given to the positive role of the laity in matters of faith. Precisely because it is the practice of the faith, and not speculative or theoretical formulations of the faith, the *sensus fidelium* deserves a hearing by theologians and hierarchy alike. But, and this is the problem today, the positive contribution of the laity is hard to determine because of the absence of adequate institutional means for expressing it and clarifying it.

Real difference
However, although both hierarchy and laity participate in the work of Christ, they do so on the basis of the real difference between their functions. To ignore the difference between hierarchy and laity in the church is to invite disastrous consequences for the reform called for by Vatican II. Fundamentally, the church has two core dimensions: the christological and the pneumatological. The church is always both, and concretely that means an interplay between its two inalienable dimensions, specific ministries and offices as well as charisms or gifts of the Spirit for all the baptised. Historically, the forms these have taken have been extremely diverse. The rediscovery by Vatican II of the equal importance of the charismatic element, so long as the

church is understood as both christological and pneumatological, opens the way today for the adoption of more democratic forms of organisation in the church itself. This is a theology that is still unfolding and is one of the surprises of the Spirit.

If the laity-versus-hierarchy model is false, so too is a model which isolates the hierarchy and reduces the voice of the laity and theologians to silent obedience. The teaching of Vatican II on the *sensus fidei*, and the positive experience of a *sensus fidelium* in the history of the church, needs to be translated today into a genuine *voice* for the laity. The only solid basis for such a voice is *dialogue*, and the hierarchy must show itself more disposed to meaningful institutions where dialogue can occur, e.g. synods. The current experience in the church, however, is one of the regular disruption of communication. The Council has already showed us the way to a church of dialogue by its ecclesiology of communion, based on a profound understanding of the church as itself a reflection of the inner-trinitarian life of the full communion of the persons of the Trinity in dialogue. The church is People of God when it is an expression of divine-human communion. Such an understanding of the church calls for more than operational institutions of dialogue. It must be based on a true 'culture of dialogue'.[1]

The hierarchy and theologians must listen to the insights of the faithful on their experience of the faith, and the historically tested forum for doing this is some form of synod which brings all parties together.

American Episcopal Initiative
As Richard Gaillardetz pointed out, in the 1980s the American Bishops modelled a promising consultation process in the way they set about producing two pastoral letters on war and peace and the economy.[2] Prior to the promulgation of both documents, extensive listening and consultation processes were facil-

---

1. See Christopher O'Donnell's entry 'Sense of the Faith – Sense of the Faithful' in his *Ecclesia: A Theological Encyclopedia of the Church* (Collegeville: Liturgical Press, 1996) 422–24. O'Donnell is very helpful in presenting the general points regarding the *sensus fidelium*.
2. Richard R. Gaillardetz, *The Church in the Making* (Mahwah, New York: Paulist Press, 2006) 97ff.

itated in open hearings, where a range of experts attended. Clearly, the bishops were taking seriously the assumption of Vatican II that all God's people and not just the hierarchy should be consulted in the process of ecclesial discernment. Building on the success of this approach, they sought to replicate it in the late 1980s when a new pastoral letter on women was being formulated. However, the Vatican intervened to block the process and prevent it from happening. As Gaillardetz tersely puts it 'Subsequent episcopal documents promulgated by the conference have not used the earlier methodology.'[3]

One can but assume that such a collaborative model was considered not only to be a dangerous innovation but also potentially problematic in that it could be interpreted as setting a dangerous precedent for episcopal leadership. Yet the work of theologians such as Küng, Schillebeeckx, Boff and Haight have all sought to make 'charism', rather than office, the constitutive starting point for understandings of ministry and order in the church.[4]

The *sensus fideliuem* is a charism that flows from the gift of the spirit in baptism and confirmation and is an expression of the presence of grace and truth, of Jesus Christ in the church which consists of the totality of believers. It is a basic means of understanding the faith and as such exercises a truth-finding and a truth-attesting function. It takes into account the faithful's experience of the world. Thus both the pope and the bishops, as well as theologians, must encourage believers to speak, and should listen to them and validate their experience. If the church reflects the inner trinitarian communion, 'because the reality of God exists as a dialogical community', then it needs communal structures of dialogue or communication. This does not reduce all three to the same function, but rather highlights the uniqueness of each one's contribution to the common witness to the faith. Thus, the hierarchical magisterium has a greater regulative role to play in formulating and teaching the faith.

---

3. Ibid., 97.
4. Hans Küng, *The Church* (New York: Image Books, 1976); Edward Schillebeeckx, *The Church with a Human Face* (New York: Crossroads, 1985); Roger Haight, *Christian Community in History*, 2 vols (New York: Continuum, 2004-5).

Theologians must exercise their rationally critical function in order to assure the credibility of the message within and beyond the confines of the church. Finally, the faithful have their contribution to make as an indispensable principle of Christian revelation, for without their witness the faith would soon lose its vitality and its ability to attract believers.

The *sensus fidelium* is a genuine criterion of theological understanding along with sacred scripture, tradition, theology and the magisterium. The latter does not establish the faith but preserves and communicates it as handed down by the community; it is dependent on the *sensus fidelium* and in that sense, is subordinate to it. As Congar put it:

> The co-operation of the faithful in the church's teaching function belongs to her life and the actual exercise of apostolic powers, not to her structural powers or acts conditioning the validity of hierarchical actions. What we find in scripture and the old tradition is the union of the hierarchical structural principle and a principle of corporate exercise. This point is so important and decisive for the very formation of the laity.[5]

This truth was to find a ringing endorsement in Article 12 of the Dogmatic Constitution of the Church which boldly confirms that 'The body of the faithful as a whole, anointed as they are by the Holy One (John 2:20) cannot err in matters of belief ... For by this sense of faith which is aroused and sustained by the Spirit of truth, God's people accepts not the word of men but the very word of God (1 Thess 2:13).'

Obviously there is significant tension in how this *sensus fidelium* is exercised in conjunction with the magisterium. Here we are confronted with an arena where one has an 'encounter and friction of intellect and authority, of reason and revelation, of the search for truth and the claims of divinely revealed truth.'[6] Newman depicts it as a battle or a duel:

> ... it is the vast Catholic body itself, and it only, which affords an arena for both combatants (the infallible authority of the

---

5. Yves Congar, *Jalons pour une théologie du laïcat*, trs Donal Attwater in 1957 as *Lay People in the Church*, p 267.
6. Thomas J. Norris, *Getting Real about Education* (Dublin: Columba Press 2006) 41.

church and private judgement or reason) in that awful never-ending duel ... Catholic Christendom is no simple exhibition of religious absolutism, but it presents a continuous picture of authority and private judgement alternately advancing and retreating as the ebb and flow of the tide.'

Legrand picks up on Newman's seminal image of a *conspiratio* which argued that there was a place for public opinion in the formal debates around matters of faith. When it is approached in this way, the proper place of public opinion can be conceded. Public opinion points to the inescapable necessity of such processes as discussion, debate, and the availability of open means of communication in the church. When these conditions are lacking, the true nature of faith-inspired consensus cannot emerge. Legrand's thesis is that the church's historical and canonically determined practice of holding synods at various levels in the church is still the best means for effecting reception and arriving at ecclesial *consensus fidelium*. Legrand's present-ation of the *sensus fidelium* has pointed to the increasingly neur-algic point in the post-conciliar church, namely, how the church determines consensus. The *consensus fidelium* is the concrete ex-pression of the whole church's faith, but efforts to form and ex-press this faith-filled consensus are weak in the church today. The situation is dangerous because some of those who constitute the consensus do not feel genuinely engaged in the process.[7]

John Millbank is a notable British Anglican theologian who would be much more cautious in his approach and he has raised interesting issues about the clamour for more democracy and consensus. In essence, he argues that society has a need for a more monarchical and aristocratic element because if you opt only for democracy you abandon the idea of objective truth or value. People are exposed to the whim of the majority.[8]

7. See 'Reception, Sensus Fidelium, and Synodal Life: An Effort at Articulation' in Reception and *Communion among Churches*, eds Herve Legrand, Julio Manzanares, and Antonio Garciay Garcia (Washington, DC: Canon Law Department of the Catholic University of America, 1997) 405–31. A reprint of *The Jurist* 57, No 1 (1997).
8. John Millbank, 'Liberality versus Liberalism' a paper delivered to the conference in Vatican City on 'The Call to Justice: the Legacy of *Gaudium et spes* Forty Years later' March 2005 at http://www.stthomas.edu/gaudium/ (downloaded 6th June 2006).

An interesting commentator on this subject is the international Anglican-Roman Catholic Dialogue (ARCIC-II) which issued its 'The Gift of Authority' in 1999. This significant document dedicated several paragraphs to the *sensus fidelium* (pars 29–31, 36, 38 and 43). In the section subtitled 'Catholicity: The Amen of the Whole Church,' the following points are made. First, the *sensus fidelium* can be found in all Christians who are struggling to be believing and practising disciples: 'In every Christian who is seeking to be faithful to Christ and is fully incorporated into the life of the church, there is a *sensus fidei*. This *sensus fidei* may be described as an active capacity for spiritual discernment, an intuition that is formed by worshiping and living in communion as a faithful member of the church' (#29).

Although the *sensus fidelium* is also revealed in the faith of the church's ordained leaders, the bishops and their presbyters have a special ministry of *episcope* that is characterised as a 'ministry of memory'. In the words of the document:

> Those who exercise *episcope* in the body of Christ must not be separated from the 'symphony' of the whole people of God in which they have their part to play. They need to be alert to the *sensus fidelium*, in which they share, if they are to be made aware when something is needed for the wellbeing and mission of the community or when some element of the tradition needs to be received in a fresh way. The charism and function of *episcope* are specifically connected to the ministry of memory, which constantly renews the church in hope. Through such ministry the Holy Spirit keeps alive in the church the memory of what God did and revealed and the hope of what God will do to bring all things into unity in Christ … The bishops, the clergy and the other faithful must all recognise and receive what is mediated from God through each other. Thus the *sensus fidelium* of the people of God and the ministry of memory exist together in reciprocal relationship (#30).

This long quotation makes clear that for the authors of 'The Gift of Authority' the *sensus fidelium* is best discerned among the committed faithful and that there is no inherent separation, but rather a mutual coordination of responsibilities, between the committed faithful and their ordained leaders.

Sensus Fidelium and Public Opinion

Vitali seeks to explain the similarities and the differences between public opinion and the *sensus fidelium*. He takes seriously the reservations of the Congregation for the Doctrine of the Faith when it writes, 'Dissent sometimes also appeals to a kind of sociological argumentation which holds that the opinion of a large number of Christians would be a direct and adequate expression of the "supernatural sense of the faith" ' (#35, quoting *LG* 12 at the end). Vitali feels that confusing the role of public opinion and the *sensus fidelium* represents a 'category mistake', though he does not use the term. Public opinion serves a useful function as a social tool in forming modern-day democracies, while the subjective-ecclesial dimension of the *sensus fidelium* aims at expressing the faith of the church as Christ's body and not at determining it. This faith is the gift of Christ and his Spirit, and so to speak of it in the terms of public opinion misunderstands its character as divine gift of truth. But does this reservation mean that there are no similarities between public opinion and the *sensus fidelium*? To say that would be to go too far in distinguishing both realities. The faith is not something static, it develops organically, though that does not mean without 'ups and downs,' progress and deviations. The human members of Christ's body are subject to the limitations of growing in human knowledge and to the breakthroughs also. In this case, public opinion can serve a useful role, as long as it is pursued not to *determine* the faith but to help in the process of *growth in understanding* the faith. That means that the faithful must attend constantly to the data of the Christian faith, while the pope and bishops, in the exercise of their pastoral magisterium, must attend to the genuine concerns, questions, and contributions of all the faithful. There is no place for 'lording it over the word of God' (see *DV* 10), whether by the church's pastors or its faithful.

The call by the magisterium that Catholics seriously consider the morality of capital punishment or the morality of resorting to modern all-out war, are but two examples of the role of the magisterium in challenging entrenched positions among many pastors, theologians, and the faithful. If public opinion can serve a useful function within the process of determining the *sensus fidelium*, then perhaps the official church needs to take more seriously the consulting of its pastors, theologians, and the faithful by conducting its own polls and gathering the necessary information for making important decisions on urgent matters, e.g. the dangerous decline in the numbers of ordained priests, etc. If there is reason to be suspicious of the methods and motives of some of the secular groups who conduct polls or interpret their results, that very fact does not absolve the official church itself from arranging for the conducting of sound polls under its direction.

Vatican II and Sensus Fidelium

The validity of the teaching of Vatican II regarding the *sensus fidelium* is no longer questioned, and it currently occupies an important place in theological reflection on some of the most basic teachings of the Council. These include the church as the People of God, the priesthood of all the faithful, the participation of all baptised believers in the three offices of Christ the prophet, priest, and king, charisms liberally bestowed by the Spirit on believers, and the call of all to active participation in the mission of the church and to holiness in one's state of life.

The *sensus fidelium* makes greater sense as a constitutive element of the believing, thinking and acting church as a whole. *Communio* ecclesiology can better correlate disparate yet interrelated elements of the church's life and activity than preconciliar ecclesiology could do: unity in diversity and richness of resources, unity of mission exercised by those with different tasks, genuine dialogue and honest communication in the assurance of an underlying unity in faith among believers. Furthermore, we need to acknowledge the emergence of pneumatology in postconciliar theology. The depths of *communio* ecclesiology are unthinkable apart from the growing importance of the Spirit in Trinitarian theology, in the contemporary theology of grace, and in ecclesiology. Pneumatology and the ecclesiology of *communio* go hand in hand.

Problematic

While accepting Vatican II's renewed stress on the *sensus fidelium*, theologians have continued to acknowledge its 'problematic' character. There remains the perennial danger of a naïve or romantic view that ignores the problems inherent in the unfulfilled or open status of the *sensus fidelium*. It is true knowledge, but knowledge that is also partial and that expresses the pilgrim character of all saving knowledge, both for the individual believer and for the whole community of believers. Awareness of this character of the *sensus fidelium* prevents Christians from claiming too much and from falling into a sense of complacency in the faith. Faith is always both project and possession. We all live today with the global dangers posed by religious fundamentalisms and by forms of terrorism that are undergirded by misplaced faith or religious convictions. Perhaps we all need to develop a healthy sense of the incompleteness of our human grasp of the ultimate Mystery that sustains us. Yet impatience with the pace of change is also a reality.

This impatience comes to expression in the groups of the faithful already referred to – the 'Petition of the People of the Church' and 'We Are the People' – and more recently in the United States, the 'Voice of the Faithful' in response to the scandals associated with sexual abuse of children and minors by priests and the role played by the bishops throughout the years of abuse. In all of these movements, and others like 'Call to Action,' one could argue that the church is being called to implement the Council's teaching on the *sensus fidelium* in a more practical way. Not only must the church give witness to the 'sense of the faithful' but also to how this 'sense of the faithful' becomes really manifest and effective in the manifestation of a 'consensus of the faithful' on what is believed and what is to be done in the church. Thus, the notion of 'consensus' expresses the public character of the underlying *sensus fidelium*. How do we arrive at such consensus? What is consensus, anyway? How should it be formulated? And what is the role of dialogue in arriving at this consensus? These are all major issues with which the church needs to actively engage as we strive to re-appropriate a key church treasure.

CHAPTER 8

Leadership and the God who lies in wait

Leadership in the church has certain inbuilt assumptions. One of the core assumptions is that formal leadership structures within the church belong to the clerical state. There has been a long and at times complicated history that has led to this reality. A foundational principle of this construct is the belief that it is primarily to this clerical group that the care of the enterprise has been entrusted. As shepherds of the flock it is their duty to assume leadership roles, protect the vision and be responsible for the direction and the major decision making about the content and governance. Called apart to mirror Christ and to follow in his footsteps, just as Christ led the disciples, so too the clerical caste is to be the religious and spiritual leadership.

This perception still holds sway in most church circles today. Yet there are signs that there is increasing dissatisfaction with this mode, with a number of organisations formed by concerned laity becoming more demanding of their rights within church governance. One of the most vocal of the new organisations is the Voice of the Faithful formed in America in the 2002. The group came into being as a way to protest about the inadequate and piecemeal response that the church had made to the child abuse scandals that rocked the Catholic population. Unhappy with the way the bishops were handling issues, they became a formidable lobby group to pressurise the clerical church to act justly, openly and honourably.

In Austria, under the platform, 'We are Church,' a petition called for a generous and caring church in which laity have a voice, bishops are appointed with local consultation, women have full equal rights, the priesthood is open to both genders, celibacy is optional, artificial birth control is clearly distinguished from abortion, and sexuality can be celebrated as God's gift. The petition drive resulted in more than 500,000 signers in a church of some 6 million. Originally, the organisers had hoped for 100,000 signatures. The movement spread. In August the Swiss conducted a poorly publicised drive which still resulted in 73,000 signatures. There are about three million Catholics in Switzerland of whom no more than 10% are practising. Like the Austrians, the Swiss called for the ordination of women and married men. Many were troubled because Bishop Hans Vogel of Basel, a young and very popular man, had resigned his position after announcing that he would soon become a father.

These may be forerunners of more robust and demanding lay groups who will not be satisfied with the lack of influence accorded to the lay voice in church governance.

Given the radical new direction in which the church was launched post Vatican II, some would believe that such a move was almost inevitable. The rediscovery of the baptismal dignity of each person and the equality of all vocations within the life of the church raised profound questions about who leads the church and how she is governed. The keys of the kingdom may be entrusted to the pope, but how he is chosen and to whom authority is subsequently delegated and how it is administered need serious consideration. Lombaerts (2006) argues that a 'withered tradition is not granted authority in modern society.'[1] Leaders need to be accountable and traditionally through the *sensus fidelium* there was a trusted mechanism for the church to assent to or to dissent from the official line of the church. To a large extent, that dimension of the magisterium has been silent or largely ignored. But perhaps the Spirit, as always, has gone ahead of us.

One of the most surprising developments in recent years has been the emergence of a host of new ecclesial movements, many of which are lay-founded and led by laymen or women.[2] They have been described as a 'providential action of the Spirit', as an 'ecclesiological novelty' and as a 'freedom of forms' by the late Pope John Paul II. Many of them are comprised of the different states of life – cleric, religious and lay – who have been led to a communal way of life under a unique charism inspired in a founder or foundress.

1. Lombaerts, Herman (Awaiting Publication, 2007)
2. Tony Hanna, *New Ecclesial Movements* (New York: Alba House, 2006).

In these new movements the leader can be drawn from any state of life. It is not assumed that it should be the cleric or the religious. This has raised difficult issues for the structures of governance in the church. For example, there is a wonderful French community called Emmanuel that has among its varied membership a host of lovely young women who are effectively living as a new form of religious life. They have not become a religious order because they do not want to separate themselves from the community, and they cannot be recognised as a religious congregation as long as they have a layperson in charge. Canon law does not yet permit this. At a seminar on these new movements in the early part of the new millennium, Cardinal Ratzinger, in response to a query on possible structural changes in the church on foot of the arrival of these new ecclesial movements, said, 'Organisation must follow life, not the other way round.'

Perhaps in these new movements there is a glimpse of where the Spirit is leading the church. Leadership is given not according to one's state in life but because of one's gifts and the needs and the discernment of the community. Against this background, and aware of the church always being in need of reform, always in need of rebuilding because she too is subject to the law of life which has stages of growth, decay, ruin and renewal, I suggest, with respect the following.

Episcopal Appointments

First of all, there is the issue of the nomination of bishops. Since the mid-nineteenth century, the selection of bishops by secular princes and by cathedral chapters has all but vanished and few would seriously advocate a return to what was obviously a very flawed system. The old method accorded far too much influence to secular authorities. Today the basic approach is one whereby the papal nuncio or delegate has major responsibility for gathering names from his personal knowledge and from consultation with people whose discernment he considers to be worthy of approach. (In effect laity are ignored.) The criteria by which men are judged to be candidates for the episcopacy 'are too focused on questions of institutional maintenance and personal agreeability and too little focused on zeal and a demonstrated capacity for counter-cultural leadership.'[3] The appointments are then discussed in the Vatican's Congregation of Bishops, which includes bishops from different regions, who make their own suggestions. The pope receives all the recommendations and makes the final choice.

Reform of Consultative Process

Although this is an improvement on what used to exist, many of the faithful would like a more open and 'democratic' process whereby names are submitted by the local church, filtered through the national or regional conference of bishops, and eventually proposed to Rome for approval or disapproval. Significantly, there should be, as an absolute minimum, an effective consultative voice for the laity. At the moment their voice is not heard or recognised. *De facto* 'the consultation process for the nunciature's terna is dominated by the bishops and those priests whom they trust or the nuncio trusts – which means that the process of consultation is heavily tilted towards those parts of the clerical bureaucracy that have a vested interest in the *status quo*.'[4] Moreover, there is a tendency to appoint only men who have at least reached their fiftieth year. This caution may be due to past flaws in some of the appointees. However, it is worth noting that while age may bring wisdom it can also bring inertia. Tradition reminds us that many of the great bishops of the past were young men when they were appointed. Saint Cyril Of Alexandria was thirty-six, Saint Ambrose was thirty-four, Saint Augustine was forty-one while Saint Francis de Sales and Saint Charles Boromeo were in their mid thirties.

The church also needs men with different gifts and talents in these pivotal roles. No Board of Directors of any significant company today would survive if all the members were lawyers or accountants or planners. They need a variety of occupational skills, personality traits and competencies. Likewise the church needs administrators, apostles, shepherds, pastors, agitators, prophets, canon lawyers, strategists etc., within its episcopal

---

3. George Wiegel, *The Courage To Be Catholic* (Basic Books: New York, 2002) 202.
4. Ibid., 203.

ranks. It is the one and the same Spirit who distributes his gifts and the church needs them all to be manifested in those who exercise leadership.

In the post-Vatican II model of church, often characterised as the People of God, it is imperative, as an issue of justice, that these deficiencies are rectified. In a truly participative church, the election of the bishop should be conducted in a way that gives the clergy and people of a diocese, i.e. the local church as such, the bishops of the province (the region), and the whole episcopal conference, effective input into the selection of the person chosen. The present system suggests a monarchical, supreme papacy above and apart from the episcopate, and does not reflect Vatican II's ecclesiology of communion at all levels of church life. It suggests an innate distrust of the ability of the local church to discern wisely who its pastor should be. Historically, in the early church bishops were elected by the clergy and the people who attended synods and councils and collaboratively engaged in participative decision-making around such key appointments. When selecting bishops today, could the starting point be a return to the practice of the first thousand years? One single process or pattern is not needed for the entire church. Is it one size fits all? Would it be unreasonable for bishops' conferences to fulfill the function of the ancient patriarchates, setting the rules not only for naming bishops but for such activities as certifying theology professors? Could synodal structures be strengthened and be seen to function everywhere, thus assuming different forms in various cultural situations? Could vigilance and responsibility replace the centralised control system that currently obtains?

Helpful Suggestions

As an initial reform, Archbishop Quinn suggests that it's inappropriate for the nuncio to make the final determination of the terna (the list of three names) sent to Rome, since priority belongs to the local episcopate. Another articulate advocate for change within the episcopacy itself is the Belgian Cardinal Daneels, who remarked: 'To impose a bishop against the majority of bishops doesn't seem very smart to me'. It does not respect the ancient principle of wisdom: 'What concerns all should be discussed and approved by all.'[5]

Daneels is particularly critical of the Curia, which he sees as being a kind of third force, a *tertium quid*, which has more than a penchant for usurping the advisory and at times legislative role of the bishops. He dislikes the way the Curia has become (in his words) 'a command organisation'.[6] To be fair, it has been reformed to some extent in that its membership is now much more international than heretofore, but much still needs to be done. The curia was developed in the twelfth century as a kind of papal court to mirror that of the emperor. It is effectively the administrative or bureaucratic arm of the papacy. Vatican II sought to reform it so that it would serve the pope and bishops in the exercise of their pastoral ministry to the universal church (*CD* #9) rather than exercise a policing function which it seems to have appropriated to itself over the centuries.

Curial Reform

For reform to happen at the practical level, conciliar structures (i.e. councils and synods) at every level of the life of the church are needed. These are structures that do not threaten the primacy of the pope in principle, but only as the primacy has been understood and practised in the second millennium, and even more narrowly since Vatican I. Cardinal Daneels proposes specifically, 'more serious consultations among the entire hierarchy on specific questions'.[7] He also proposes surrounding the pope with what he calls 'a council to the crown', made up of six or seven bishops or cardinals from around the world with the function of 'counsellors'.[8] The centralisation of ecclesial power is quite a recent phenomenon. In 1829 there were 646 diocesan bishops in the Latin Church, 555 of whom were appointed with significant state influence, 67 by diocesan chapters or their equivalent, with the pope only appointing 24. It was the *Code of Canon Law* of 1917

---

5. Godfried, Cardinal Daneels, 'On Papal Primacy and Decentralisation', *Origins* (October 30, 1997) 339-341, and *Doctrine and Life* 47:10 (December 1997) 581.
6. Ibid., 582.
7. Ibid., 579.
8. Ibid., 582.

that claimed that the right to appoint bishops was an integral part of papal primacy. It was hoped that the Second Vatican Council would reclaim a stronger authoritative role for the Episcopal College to redress an over emphasis on papal primacy. Xavier Rynne, an astute commentator on the Council, wrote in 1996 that the most important achievement of Vatican II 'has unquestionably been the proclamation of episcopal collegiality, the principle that the bishops form a college and govern the church together with the pope who is their head ... the new doctrine is bound to influence the exercise of (papal) authority in practice, particularly if Pope Paul's plans for the reform of the Roman Curia and the establishment of the Synod of Bishops are fully carried out.'[9] In effect, the plans were tinkered with and little actual change has occurred. The Curia remains largely unaccountable to the episcopate and the Synods as currently configured are little more than instruments of papal power.

Power of Bishops
The role of the episcopal synod had been raised at Vatican II to reclaim a lost authority and prestige for the bishops. Many of the advocates for such a structure envisaged something similar to the Eastern churches' practice of a permanent standing synod of bishops who have a deliberative authority to assist the pope in his governance. This would make the curia responsible to this standing synod and would neutralise their power. Moreover, it would strengthen significantly the role of the episcopacy and redress the anomaly whereby the Roman Curia *de facto* has authority over the bishops. Pope John Paul II's *Apostolos Suos* (*motu proprio* – a document issued on the pope's own initiative) in 1998 offered a historical review of episcopal conferences. In one sense he dammed them with faint praise in that he acknowledged the contributions they had made to the life of the church but he underlined their limited doctrinal authority. *Apostolos Suos* demands that only if three conditions are fulfilled can bishops exercise the ordinary magisterium, namely, a document issued in plenary session, with unaminous approval or at least a two thirds majority and a formal *recognitio* from Rome.

---

9. Xavier Rynne, *The Fourth Session* (London: Faber & Faber, 1966) 257.

Proposal

To give an enhanced role to episcopal conferences and to appoint a standing synod of bishops would seem to be a logical step in the rediscovery of the authentic role of the bishop. Likewise, there needs to be a rediscovery of the former role of the papacy as the court of final appeal, and a fresh examination of its present role where the pope is portrayed as the chief theologian of the church. This is not only unrealistic, given the range of issues that need attention, but it again undermines the bishop's role of teacher and it is disrespectful of his competence and ignores his acumen around local issues.

Marian model as a New Paradigm

Vatican II caused a radical rethink about this understanding of the church and there was a call for a return to the founding intention of the church where all its members were seen as equal. This in turn encouraged a profound sense of belonging and responsibility for the welfare and the development of the church's mission. Vatican II rediscovered the Marian model of church as the *leitmotif*. This is the life-giving church that births Christ in all kinds of new and unexpected Bethlehems. Often it is the simple and hidden church of Nazareth where Christ plays in a thousand places. It is maternal and compassionate, bringing Christ to life in diverse milieus, transforming hearts and minds. It is the way of being church *par excellence*. Rather than being subservient to the institutional or Petrine model of church, it is called to be the prophetic voice that beckons the institution to embrace and follow. The Petrine is called to serve the Marian, not the other way round. These two aspects of the church are co-essential but the Marian model is the authentic way of being church. The institution is called to serve life. The Marian has priority and the role of the Petrine is to discern where authentic life is taking place, to protect and nurture that life.

'A Marian church is a church which makes a choice for compassion and competition, an option for relationship over dogmatism; for humility over power; for service over dominance. It is a church which pushes its boundaries to include all, rather than one which defines its boundaries to contain the chosen. And it is a church which includes the feminine in its attitudes, which can too easily become over-masculine. The church with a Marian face does not feel the need to create bigger and better things to ensure that God is properly honoured. It is a church that understands that small things can be, and often are, the most significant things.'[10]

Leader and Servant

Leadership is an ethic, a gift of oneself to a common cause, a higher calling. The essence of leadership is not giving or doing things or even providing visions. It is simply offering oneself and one's spirit, just being of service to others within the community. The gifts of authorship, love, power, and significance, work only when they are freely given and freely received. Leaders cannot give what they do not have, or lead to places they have never been.

Christ chose the way of emptiness, the way of utter *kenosis* as starkly depicted by his chosen helplessness on the cross. He laid down his life freely, poured it out it in the ultimate service of redemptive love. Not only did he wash our feet with water but he washed our sins with the cleansing gift of his very blood. Such a model of servant leadership is radical and shocking. It places before all aspirant leaders who would undertake positions of leadership and authority within the church a stark template.

Henri Nouwen

One churchman who took this challenge seriously was Henri Nouwen. A gifted theologian and writer, his work had reached a wide and an appreciative audience and he revelled in his teaching career at Harvard where his many skills were deeply appreciated by the best and brightest young minds who sat at his feet. Yet, there was a growing dissatisfaction within himself. He had a sense of emptiness and a gnawing realisation that the kingdom he was building was his own. Grace and prayer led him unexpectedly to surrender his prestigious career and join with the L'Arche community of Jean Vanier. It was a radical and at times painful move, one that brought him from the ivory

---

10. Craig Larkin, 'A Certain Way: An exploration of Marist Spirituality.'

tower to the coalface of humanity. Among the simple and un-affected members of the L'Arche community he underwent a steep and profound learning curve that challenged him, stretched him and almost broke him. Ultimately it led him to a profound sense of peace and fulfillment among the poor, the *anawim*, the forgotten little people who taught him just to be. He was led to a place where he would rather not go but one where he found Christ waiting for him and welcoming him. Nouwen came to see that no one gets to heaven without a reference from the poor. Leaders who operate out of an unfulfilled power-need damage not only those whom they lead but also themselves. Henri Nouwen speaks eloquently about the temptation in all of us to seek power.[11] He reminds us that it was the third and perhaps the most insidious of all the temptations that Jesus confronted in the desert. The demon sought to deter Christ from his mission with the promise to 'give you all the kingdoms of the world in their splendour,' Matthew 4:9. It is a perennial weakness at the heart of man's flawed humanity and it is not surprising that, throughout Christian history, many of our leaders have often succumbed to this third temptation of power, whether it is eco-nomic, political, moral or even spiritual.

Daniel Berrigan

Another modern day churchman is Daniel Berrigan, the emin-ent anti-war campaigner, who speaks of a similar moment of epiphany in his own life's journey. He had visited a young para-plegic man in hospital. Such was the scale of his injuries that the patient was incapable of any form of communication. The young man lay there in utter silence apart from his breathing. As Berrigan visited and watched, he had a sense of how this was a metaphor for the way that Christ chooses to be present in our world. Silent and helpless, he waits for us to be stirred by his kenotic presence.

Can we become inspired to be present for others, to lay down our grandiose illusions about ourselves, to tame the ego's insati-able lust for power and recognition? Can we become leaders like the one we seek to follow? Can we lay down our lives?

11. Henri Nouwen, *In the name of Jesus* (New York: The Crossroads Publishing Company) 76.

One of the subtlest temptations about the use of power is that it is needed to proclaim the gospel. The opposite is often the case. The lessons of history teach us that such rationalisations have resulted in inquisitions, crusades, enslavements of tribal peoples, opulent lifestyles and lavish church trappings. It has also caused a fortress mentality concerned about protecting positions and authority and power. It was the dominant controlling motif of the church for much of the last century.

Power is attractive because it substitutes (badly) for the difficult task of love. Intimacy is always risky because it involves one in the messiness and the vulnerability of relationships that stretch and tax beyond the comfort zone. Intimacy and love make demands on all. They require work and negotiation and understanding and compromise and sacrifice and forgiveness. They require surrender and letting go and sometimes letting be. They mean a certain dying to self. They cost big time! Power dispenses with most of these demands. As Nouwen put it, 'It seems easier to be God than to love God, easier to control people than to love people, easier to own life than to love life.'[12] The temptation to power is at its strongest when intimacy is at its weakest. 'The long history of the church is the history of people succumbing to the temptation to choose power over love, control over the cross, being a leader over being led.'[13]

Genuine Consultation

At the outset of the third millennium for Christianity, and as the church responds spiritually and intellectually to the passing of the eventful pontificate of John Paul II, one antidote to the abuse of power will be a recovery of the role of the *sensus fidei* in the church. This conciliar teaching has tremendous implications for the concrete form that the church in the third millennium will assume. Yet these implications remain largely untapped. One of the tasks of the future church will surely be to continue to clarify, but especially to foster, the 'sense of the faith' and to challenge all believers to become actively involved in defining the faith for themselves personally and for the entire community of the faith-

---

12. Ibid., 77.
13. Ibid.

ful. In this great undertaking, we shall have to pay much greater attention to the relationships among the *sensus fidei*, the *sensus fidelium*, and the *consensus fidelium*.

The consultative structures of the church are still only 'recommended' and 'advisory'. They do not necessarily facilitate lay participation in real decision-making. Such participation, as well as its authority, are dependent on the individual bishop or parish priest, and may be dismantled at will. Denis Edwards sees this participation by laity in the decision-making of the church as one of the great challenges of the third millennium. In Edwards' view, 'We need to embrace decisively a move away from all forms of clericalism towards an understanding of baptismal equality.'[14]

Further, it is anomalous in the extreme that, even in those areas considered by the Council to be the areas of expertise of the laity, e.g. work, marriage and family, laity does not have any more than advisory or auditory roles. Even in the great Synod of 1987, discussing the very role of laity in the church, lay people were only present as auditors. And while there was consultation prior to the synod, it seems to have been patchy in coverage, and uncertain as to whether any of it survived the process to be integrated in the output. Moreover, the Pontifical Council for the Laity, supposedly the lay voice within the church structures, is seen by many as being less than lay in its composition and as focusing its attention mainly on fringe charismatic movements rather than on genuine lay apostolate movements.[15] Even the 1983 *Code of Canon Law* revision, while promising much, delivered something short of the expectations raised by the Council. It left ambiguities and uncertainties and threw little light on the 'secular' identity of the laity. As Herbert Haag described it, 'as far as the new Code is concerned, the Catholic Church is and remains a clerical church.'[16]

---

14. Denis Edwards, *Called to be Church in Australia* (Sydney: St Paul Publications,1987) 58.

15. See The Cardijn Internet Site, 'The Council of the Laity Makes Way for the Pontifical Council for the Laity,' www.cardijn.net/1997-mc-2-roussel/page4.htm. (Accessed11/09/02.)

16. See Herbert Haag, *Upstairs Downstairs: Did Jesus Want a Two-Class Church?* (New York: Crossroad Press, 1997) 30.

Recognition for the Sole Traders

Critics of the church's authoritarianism (both real and imag-
ined) emanates from the fact that our rapidly changing society
in which the church finds itself, 'is much more likely to see reality
in terms of a sea of influences rather than a structure of orders.'[17]
There is a growing sense of alienation from institutional structures. So many people today don't experience a sense of belonging in the church. As one person explained it to me, she said she
felt 'like a sole trader' in terms of her own spirituality. There are
a host of such 'sole traders' who are establishing their own solo
or small-group circles of faith which are embarking on a 'do it
yourself' kind of search for truth. They don't appear on the
radar of the official church structures nor are they finding life
within the old dispensation. Their existence and their rapid
expansion raises huge pastoral issues for the church and how it
exercises its authoritative role.

My work has taken me to many parts of Ireland and one of
the questions I pose to people is 'Where do you find life; what
nurtures your own spiritual journey?' Some, a minority, will
speak of the institutional church as their source of life but the
vast majority speak of prayer groups, support groups, personal
study, reading, poetry, music, art, family, nature, friends as their
daily contact or conduit with the divine. Non-acceptance of the
institutional authority produces what can best be described as a
kind of moral withdrawal, manifested in silence, a reduced
enthusiasm or participation in any liturgical events or a more
strident questioning of the authority's mandate over a particular
issue.

In seeking to find solutions to divisive issues in the local
church today, authority cannot focus on strong calls for
uniformity or seek to dilute the notion of an authoritative presence. A balance must be sought between these two polarities. As
the German theologian, Heinrich Fries noted, 'It is … not at all
the case that authority is universally rejected today. It is accepted

---

17. Charles E. Curran, 'Responsibility in Moral Theology: Centrality,
Foundations and Implications for Ecclesiology', in James A. Coriden,
ed., *Who Decides for the Church? Studies in Co-Responsibility* (Hartford,
CT: The Canon Law Society of America,1971) 141.

and even welcomed when it argues convincingly on the basis of insights of faith and proves itself competent.'[18]

It is clear as we move into an increasingly volatile milieu that we need the strength of the universal church to maintain, in the global context, the voice of faith. Yet we also need, in the rapid disappearance of old certainties and an increasing rootlessness in people, the identity and support of the local faith community.

---

18. Heinrich Fries, *Suffering From the Church: Renewal or Restoration?* trs Arlene Anderson Swidler and Leonard Swidler (Collegeville: Liturgical Press, 1995) 46. See also Gadamer, *Truth and Authority*, 279: 'Authority cannot actually be bestowed but is earned and must be earned if someone is to lay claim to it. It rests on acknowledgement and hence on an act of reason itself which, aware of its own limitations, trusts to the better insights of others.'

CHAPTER 9

Bringing it all back Home

I have a favourite little modern day parable about the fellow from the town and his companion from the country who are walking along a busy street during rush hour. Suddenly, the country fellow stops and says to his friend, 'Did you hear that?'

'What?' says the townsman.

'The sound of the cricket,' replies the countryman.

'You must be joking,' says the townsman. 'How could you hear anything like that in the midst of all this noise?'

The countryman stops, bends down and feels around the busy pavement and picks up a little green cricket in his cupped hands.

'Well, I'll be damned,' says the townsman. 'How on earth did you hear that?'

'Watch this,' says the countryman. He takes a coin out of his pocket, flips it and lets it fall to the pavement where it makes a slight ringing noise. Immediately, in the midst of all the hustle and bustle, despite the cacophony of traffic and people, a number of people stop and look for the coin.

'See that,' says the countryman. 'It all depends on what your ear is attuned to.'

As I draw my thoughts on this topic to a close, I would like to make some observations about how all of this affects the local Irish church. In so many ways it all depends on what your ear is attuned to. First, I need to sketch the context as I see it.

We are in a moment of seismic change. The landscape of our country is being altered in truly remarkable ways. Ireland is reimagining itself! The political landscape has been transformed by the Good Friday Agreement which is finally bearing fruit. Implacable adversaries have found a way to listen to and to work with each other. They are creating a new kind of music together, albeit tentatively and cautiously.

Our economic landscape is mindboggling in scope and potential. The grinding poverty of much of the last century has given way to a modern, vibrant, confident and affluent reality which is normative for most of our people. This has made us a land of destination rather than emigration, and we now play host to a burgeoning panoply of people from all nations and creeds who have come to share in this economic transformation. In the words of Yeats, 'All's changed, changed utterly, a terrible beauty is born.' We are listening to a new and beautiful chorus.

Garret FitzGerald produced a very interesting paper for Boston College in 2005 and what follows in the next few paragraphs are drawn from his statistics and some of his analysis. He states that from the 1960s onward, Irish society has undergone startling changes in sexual mores. The proportion of births outside of marriage rose from 2 per cent of the total in 1965 to 31 per cent in 2003, at which level it seems recently to have stabilised. Today 10 per cent of Irish pregnancies are aborted in Britain each year. For much of the past decade, over half of all first pregnancies have been non-marital. The Irish rate of non-marital births is much higher than in other European Catholic countries, including Spain, Portugal, and Italy, and is also higher than in Germany and the Netherlands.

Another recent development has been an increase in the proportion of civil marriages, from just under 4 per cent in 1991 to 18 per cent in 2002. Some of this increase reflects the sharp rise during that period in the proportion of the population registered as non-Roman Catholic or having no religion, a subgroup that grew from 6 per cent in 1991 to nearly 10 per cent in 2002, mainly due to immigration. But the shift toward civil marriage also suggests a significant change in the marriage practices of Catholics. Since the legalisation of divorce a decade ago, the ratio of divorces to marriages has risen to 17 per cent (in 2005).

Changes in religious attitudes, that took several centuries to develop elsewhere in Europe, have in Ireland all occurred within the past four decades. Since the 1960s, there has been a huge erosion of religious practice, so much so that some observers now speak of a post-Christian Ireland.

Weekly Mass attendance among Catholics has declined from higher than 90 per cent in the 1960s to an estimated 50 per cent, and in some working-class Dublin suburbs, to which families have relocated from older more established neighbourhoods, attendance is down to 5-10 per cent. In rural areas, weekly Mass attendance remains quite high, but there, also, it has fallen off. This downward trend accelerated rapidly during the 1980s and 1990s and was well-advanced even before clerical pedophilia emerged as a major scandal about a decade ago.

A convergence of factors is responsible for this dramatic development. Some portion of it has been born of broad cultural and social changes in Ireland and elsewhere. Other portions can be traced to pronouncements and circumstances within the Catholic Church, and more specifically within the Irish Catholic Church. The 2006 census revealed that 3.68 million Irish people declare themselves Catholic, out of a total population of 4.6 million. What the term 'Catholic' means is uncertain, in that many of those do not attend Mass or the sacraments on a regular basis but they still retain an emotional or historical connection with the Catholic legacy.

Some of these 3.68 million are new emigrants, mainly from Poland and other eastern European countries. They bring a new dynamism and zealous commitment to the practice of their faith. Others belong to groups such as born again Christians, charismatics, political action groups, co-counselling groups, bible discussion groups, and self-help groups of all kinds. The more disorderly and uncontrollable Christianity they herald, while it may be a necessary supplement to the traditional structures which remain necessary for the stable functioning of the Christian community, creates new challenges and problems for the church. Inter-denominational communities, or simple 'human communities' with a religious tinge, are also beginning to emerge here and there, and they promise to bring a clearer perspective and fresher air to the spiritual quest of the Irish people.

In 2003 there were nine ordinations for the whole of Ireland, eight in 2004 and eight in 2005. In 2005, for the first time in its history, the Archdiocese of Dublin didn't have a single candidate for ordination, and in the whole archdiocese there was a single priest under the age of 30. In a country that once used to export thousands of priests and nuns and brothers, African and Vietnamese priests are now a familiar sight.

The major pastoral problem of the Irish Catholic Church is that very many people, including clergy, no longer know why they continue to be Catholics. The meaning of the gospel has become veiled or, even when that is not the case, the link between the gospel and the activities of the church remains disquietingly obscure. The focal point of this religious unease is perhaps the celebration of the Eucharist but that too has become problematic. At one level, the Mass is fundamentally reassuring because it is at the core of what we understand to be the essence of Catholicism. However, over reliance on it can and does have disadvantages. With a few notable exceptions, it is largely a monologue conducted by a principal 'actor' and a supporting 'cast' that plays a very minor 'walk-on role'. There is no occasion for disruption, spurts or failures of creativity, or even real communication apart from the stylised sermon-slot. Renewal of the Mass demands a total renewal of Catholic life: better art and architecture, better theology, a greater capacity for emotional and spiritual expression. But above all what it demands is a learning attitude towards religion, including a willingness to expose and share one's doubt, anxiety and questioning. As long as we feel we have it all wrapped up, the Mass will continue to be a routine, stifling the emergence of any word from the Lord.[1]

One of the great commentators on the church over the last fifty years has been Fr Enda McDonagh. His scholarship and spiritual acumen has greatly enriched the life of the church but those same gifts have also challenged the church. In his loyal critique of the church he speaks of a 'spiritual deafness', either an inability to hear or a blatant refusal to hear. He lays this accusation largely at the feet of the clerical church, not with any sense of pique but with sadness and a certain resignation. Their ears are attuned to a different message.The reason is the petrified power-structures which have refused the laity any effective voice in the affairs of the church. These structures allow communication in one direction only. The tragic result is a confused and frustrated laity, unable to celebrate the Eucharist in a communal way or to communicate their faith to their children.

---

1. Garret FitzGerald, *The Role of Humanae Vitae* (Boston College Mag., Fall, 2006).

Local Episcopal Appointments

There is a view abroad that appointments to the episcopacy in Ireland, as elsewhere, have increasingly come to be decided on the basis of the willingness of candidates to accept and defend *Humanae Vitae*. This was an encyclical issued in 1968 defending the church's opposition to birth control within marriage. The conclusions of the encyclical blatantly disregarded the considered expert opinion of the majority of the group of Catholic experts who included committed and faithful Catholic married laity. Many would see the subsequent fallout from this decision as the crucial moment when many Catholic laity lost confidence in the authority of the magisterium.

With the declining pool of entrants to the priesthood and an apparent veto on dissenters, there is the danger that the intellectual level of the church hierarchy in Ireland will fail to keep pace with the rapidly rising educational level of the laity. Again it would appear that results of diocesan consultations on nominations to the episcopacy have come to be so persistently ignored that it has almost seemed as if that process were being used simply to identify whom not to appoint. This has created a gulf between much of the laity – together with many of the clergy – and the bishops. Moreover, the consultative procedures adopted for screening potential candidates is so clandestine, at least in terms of assessing the lay perspective, that one can only deduce that whoever is being 'sounded out' is part of a very select few. In today's canon law, the laity's role in the selection of bishop is reduced to selective consultation left to the discretion of the papal legate (c. 377, §3); this only barely acknowledges the longstanding ideal of participation by the clergy and laity in the choice of their bishop.

I have been involved actively in my church as an adult for over thirty years and I have a wide and extensive range of mature associates across Ireland who are deeply committed to church. None of us has ever been consulted on any episcopal appointment. I wonder who actually is?

The testimony of the early church confirms a widespread conviction regarding the necessity for local participation in the selection of the bishop. For most of the church's history, both the laity and the clergy had a role in the episcopal selection process.

In the ancient church, the laity directly participated in the selection of their bishop. As the church grew, only the more important lay persons, wealthy or powerful persons, participated directly. In the Middle Ages kings and other noble persons were influential and often played the decisive role in the choice of a bishop. By the twelfth century, in reaction to abuses that resulted from control by secular rulers, Episcopal elections began to be reserved more to the clergy of the diocese; the laity thenceforth were excluded from participation, except for some secular rulers who maintained their privileges.

In any objective assessment of the development away from the participation of the local church in the appointment of the bishop, it is difficult to avoid the conclusion that political rather than theological factors were responsible. The more ancient practice of local participation of the faithful would appear to have been grounded not in pragmatic political realities, as clearly was the case when their participation later diminished, but in a conviction regarding what would later be called the *sensus fidelium*.

While Christians of the early church held that bishops were chosen by God, they also believed that God's choice could be discerned through the consent of the people. Consequently, any reform of canon law should attend to this value, which corresponds to the church's self-understanding as the 'people of God'. The universal canon law of the Latin church should seek to restore to the faithful a greater role in the selection process, at least by some mandatory consultation, in every kind of selection process that may be permitted.

Enda McDonagh has suggested that 'a clean break with the Christendom mentality is necessary,' bringing 'an end to clericalism, to the caste system of bishops, priests and religious, with their power and privileges.' 'Bishops', says McDonagh, should be 'chosen as in the past by the believing community they are to serve, while confirmed in the unity of the whole church by local bishops and by the church's traditional symbol of universal unity, the Bishop of Rome.' A thousand years ago, the church was insistent on such ecclesiastical democracy. Why not again in the third millennium?

Clericalism fosters the idea that the advancement of the laity comes from admitting them to 'ministries' and allowing them to *do* things (read at Mass, distribute Communion, etc.) that only clerics formerly could do. It's like taking children to a fire station and letting them wear the firefighters' hats. The clericalist culture is variously described as a caste system, a fraternity, a club. All of these terms fit. Russell Shaw is particularly trenchant in his comments:

> In a special way, however, clericalism is rooted in the idea that in whatever pertains to religion, it is the right and the responsibility of clerics to make the decisions and give the orders, and the job of lay people to carry them out. At a deep level it is spiritual snobbery, reflecting the assumption that the clerical state, in and of itself, makes clerics spiritually superior to the laity. A mistaken idea of vocation is at work here – the idea that the calling to ordained ministry is superior to all other vocations.[2]

Conclusion

The local church is where most people encounter the church. It is the locus of ministry, liturgy and evangelisation for most of us. We may value the larger reality when we discover the splendour of the universal church on a World Youth Day, or on the election of a new pope, or on pilgrimage to some shrine or to a saint's tomb. However, it is in the immediate, local context that we taste and touch, see, hear and smell the church. For most of us, this is where we establish roots and a sense of belonging. Sadly, many find the local an inhospitable place, one where it is difficult to find even a foothold of belonging.

Psychologists such as Maslow speak of the need for humans to make a contribution in order to attain full, mental and social maturity. When the church denies people the opportunity to make a worthwhile contribution to the life of their church, it stymies its own potential and does an injustice to the People of God motif. In many cases half, if not more, of the believing community have been denied genuine opportunities to bring their full array of gifts and talents to the church. I am speaking, of course, of women.

Systematically, they have been denied equal rights within

2. Russell Shaw, 'Clericalism and Sex Abuse', *America*, 3 June 2002.

the meaningful structures of the church and, despite papal apologies for offences committed against women in the past by the church, it would appear that little is being done to rectify the situation. The newly restored permanent diaconate programme is for men only, despite obvious scriptural and historical proof that it was open to women for over ten centuries. The norms as outlined in *Institutionis Diaconorum Permanentiarium* exclude women on the grounds that it could increase expectation of priestly ordination for women. It is more than a little ironic that the same argument is not used in regard to married men. Language is another critical means of exclusion. Documents such as *Liturgiam authenticam* in 2001completely obliterate female references from the prayers and hymns of the church. Women deserve better than this. They have a much more significant contribution to make if they are given a legitimate and effective role in church discernment and governance.

Hope

Yet there are signs of hope. In an acknowledgement that would have previously been unimaginable, the Archbishop of Dublin, Diarmuid Martin, recently told the National Priests' Conference that 'priests can be extremely authoritarian, arrogant, and self-minded', and he urged them to foster a 'humble, listening church' at the parish level and above (*Irish Times*, 29 September 2004).

In the Armagh diocese on the feast of the Ascension, 2007, Archbishop Sean Brady circulated a finely crafted pastoral letter to all his people outlining the need for parish reconstruction. In it he referred to the Vatican II reclamation of the role of the laity as a right and a responsibility of baptism. He also spoke of the rapid decline in the number of priests, both of which herald a new challenge and opportunity. He has issued an invitation for all parishioners to become involved in a consultative process that will commence later this year. It appears to be a real and genuine effort at consultative dialogue and it offers a genuine possibility of productive and collaborative decision-making. In the same letter, the archbishop spoke of the need to 'engage lay people increasingly in pastoral and administrative leadership and ministries in parish communities'. We could be on the brink of a new reality where the collective gifts of the body, regardless of one's state in life, are brought into the vineyard.

Respecting authority means looking afresh at the gifts it brings, to see it not as an ogre or a kind of arrogant bully but as a God-given gift to protect eternal truths. Exercised properly, it brings order and stability and vision and imagination. We badly need those gifts in our church today at all levels and in all states of life. We also need, critically, a respectful authority, one that has the courage to revisit procedures and structures in the light of the *quaneh*, the divine measuring rod. It needs to become a listening church which recognises anew the *sensus fidelium*. Authority needs to respond with integrity to some of the dissent that is being expressed, not by cranks or disaffected minorities, but by many of the committed educated lay faithful who are increasingly skeptical of some church structures that unduly protect an outdated anachronistic model.

A Certain Messiness
Real consultative dialogue, genuine listening and collaboration, authentic partnership with the laity, is difficult to achieve because it is time-consuming, frustrating and downright messy. Relationships take time to form, trust takes time to be established, listening can be very taxing and trusting that someone else might make a better job of leading in certain circumstances than me requires deep humility and more than a little letting go. The clerical church has to learn a new way of being, a new kind of emptiness, a new way of calling people not out of positions of authority but out of profound weakness. Such leadership can only emerge out of a deep prayer base.

In her book, *Learning to Lead from your Spiritual Center*, (Nashville, TN: Abingdon Press, 1996) Patricia Brown wrote:

> Central to my leadership is the nurturing and formation of my spirit. It is a spirit not closeted or closed off to itself, but intricately woven throughout my relationship with God, who is the Divine Centre, and therefore ultimately woven to others. As I care for my spiritual wellbeing, I have come to realize that what I offer as a leader first arises from who I am. Leadership is not something 'out there', somehow separate from me. If I am to lead in ways that evidence my faith and

do not betray those I have been entrusted to serve, I must lead from a spirit-filled center (p 10-11).

Brown (1996) further stated:

The failure of leaders to deal with their own souls, their inner life, is deeply troubling not only for themselves but also for other persons in the misery they cause. Only when leaders begin to nurture their own spirits will they be able to give the sustaining leadership needed for difficult, stressful times. Leaders have a particular responsibility to know what is going on inside their souls (p 11).

Conclusion

Vatican II was an unexpected surprise of the Spirit. It re-oriented the church both to a ressourcement and an *aggiornamento*, simultaneously a return to sources and to an updating to meet the needs of the modern world. As T. S. Eliot once pointed out, the church is subject to the laws of life in that she too experiences birth, growth and decay. She must always be rebuilding and the structures she establishes should be at the service of life. We can be tempted to think that we are the architects of this building but we are merely the workers. The genius of the architect's vision is always somewhere beyond us. God too is always ahead of us, waiting with his own detailed plans, amending our mistakes and calling us constantly to follow his blueprint. Authority is a key building block in his plan. Ultimately it is his own divine authority entrusted in a large measure to the hierarchical church. He will judge with his own *quaneh* those to whom power and authority have been given. Of those to whom more has been given, more will be asked.